Contents

Contents

Introduction

The two world wars of the twentieth century never cease to arouse emotion, capture the public imagination and provoke a lively historical debate. The First World War (1914–18), largely a European conflict, left over 8 million combatants dead and was dubbed by contemporaries as the 'war to end all wars'. The Second World War (1939–45), a truly global conflict, left over 45 million dead, and evokes the dreadful images of the Holocaust and Hiroshima. It is usual for the origins of these two world wars to be examined separately. However, this book examines them in a single volume, which aims to provide a detailed analysis of the key events leading to both wars, an original and wide-ranging examination of the historical debate surrounding them, and a wide selection of primary documents on major issues. It is not the purpose of this book to provide a new theory on the origins of the wars, nor to examine the wars in comparative terms, but it is hoped that the reader will seek out elements of continuity, explore comparisons, and evaluate the different interpretations and counter-interpretations which are considered during the course of this study.

Any exploration of the origins of war must keep in mind several important factors. Power lies at the heart of nearly every explanation of why nations go to war. The influence of powerful leaders, their aims, policies and decisions are crucial to any discussion of the origins of war. A harsh or lenient peace treaty is a further factor which can promote peace or encourage war. There is a clear link between a breakdown of diplomacy and the outbreak of war. However, the most crucial factor in promoting war or peace is the prevailing balance of power between nations. It is clear that an ineffective balance of power encourages war, and a rough equilibrium of power between nations is an aid to peace. Even so, the origins of the First and Second World Wars are viewed here as unique, growing out of a particular set of circumstances, which cannot be explained by reference to any one single theory or factor.

The discussion which follows is structured in the following way. The first two chapters deal with the origins of the First World War. Chapter 1 sets the origins of the First World War in the context of long-term developments, most notably the rise of Germany, the surge of imperialism, the growth of alliances and the spread of nationalism, and relates how these underlying factors influenced the July Crisis of 1914. Chapter 2 provides an original and extensive analysis of the changing nature of the historical debate on the origins of the First World War. The final three chapters concentrate on the origins of the

Second World War. Chapter 3 provides a detailed exploration of the evolution of international affairs from 1914 to 1933. In Chapter 4, the unfolding global crisis from 1933 to 1941, when Germany, Italy and Japan undermined the peace settlement, is fully explored. Finally, Chapter 5 offers a critical survey of the vast historical debate on the origins of the Second World War, including a detailed exploration of all the key problem areas.

The book also contains three in-depth document case studies, using a wide range of primary documents, on the July Crisis of 1914, the Paris Peace Conference of 1919, and key events leading to the Second World War. In addition, there is a detailed set of notes and references which are designed to indicate more detailed sources on a wide range of important issues, as well as a useful bibliography.

1 The origins of the First World War, 1871–1914

The outbreak of the First World War in 1914 grew out of a short-term crisis in the Balkans, but any attempt to understand its origins must take account of a number of long-standing developments. For much of the nineteenth century, the major European powers maintained a balance of power. However, between 1871 and 1914 a number of factors served to undermine international stability. First, European powers saw international relations as a battle for survival and as a source of status, and engaged in a fresh outburst of imperialism in Africa and Asia. Second, the rise of Germany in central Europe aroused fear and encouraged the growth of alliances. Third, the expansion of national groups demanding self-determination threatened old empires. The final ingredient which brought war were the fatal decisions of the political leaders during the July Crisis of 1914 in the Balkans. The First World War was really the culmination of a long-drawn-out crisis within the European system.[1]

The rise of Germany

The rise of Germany was a primary factor which produced tension among the major European powers. The victory of Prussia over France in 1871 concluded the unification of Germany and created a new power at the heart of Europe. As German unification came about – through a combination of crafty diplomacy, industrial strength and military might – this produced anxiety. Contemporaries called it the 'German Question'. It revolved around how Germany would behave as the most powerful military and economic power in a reshaped Europe. Fear of Germany served to encourage unease and affected the foreign-policy decisions of Germany's major European rivals.

The startling growth of German power lay at the heart of these concerns. The German population soared from 49 to 66 million between 1890 and 1914, and the economy grew faster than that of any other country in Europe. In 1914, Germany's steel output was higher than that of Britain, France and Russia combined and coal production had risen to second position behind Britain. The prominence of science and technology in the school curriculum gave Germany a notable lead in new, 'high-tech' industries. Germany's industrial strength was used to increase its military strength. The German army, organised on the basis of conscription, was tactically sophisticated, highly trained and well equipped. German naval expansion ensured that Germany's fleet rose from being the sixth largest to the second largest in the world.[2]

The foreign policy of the new Germany, dominated by Otto von Bismarck, the first chancellor of Germany from 1871 to 1890, was designed to reassure Europe that Germany was a 'satisfied' power, with no intention of disrupting the delicate European balance of power. This ingenious style of diplomacy secured a dominant position for Germany in European affairs through the formation of a delicate system of treaties and alliances, which often contained secret clauses.[3] In 1872, the League of the Three Emperors (or *Dreikaiserbund*), consisting of Germany, Russia and Austria-Hungary, was formed. This was followed by the Dual Alliance in 1879 between Germany and Austria-Hungary, which promised mutual assistance in the event of war with Russia. Bismarck believed that the agreement would help restrain the aims of Austria-Hungary in the Balkans, but it had the opposite effect, and encouraged Austria-Hungary to take a bolder stand against Balkan nationalism. The diplomatic position of Germany was further strengthened in Bismarck's time by the formation of a military alliance with Italy in 1882, dubbed the Triple Alliance (of Germany, Austria-Hungary and Italy).

It is now apparent that Bismarck was never firmly committed to his Triple Alliance partners. In 1887, for example, he signed the secret Re-insurance Treaty with Russia, without the knowledge of Austria-Hungary or Italy, which pledged Russian neutrality in the event of a German attack on France, German neutrality in the event of a Russian attack on Austria-Hungary (a strange clause, given the terms of the Dual Alliance), and a promise that Germany would support Russia's interests in the Balkans. This diplomatic double-dealing was designed to give Germany maximum flexibility and a number of diplomatic options in the event of any international crisis, but it raised suspicions in Austria-Hungary, Russia and Italy. But it seems that Bismarck's duplicity was designed to ensure a peaceful outcome to any future international problems.[4]

The Bulgarian Crisis and the Balkan problem

Bismarck's desire to be the public ally of Austria-Hungary and the secret ally of Russia foundered during the course of the Bulgarian Crisis of the late nineteenth century. Bulgaria, a group of small, semi-independent states, was one of the most explosive and poorly governed parts of the Ottoman Empire. The key cause of instability was the existence of a wide range of nationalist groups agitating for religious toleration and self-government. In 1876, a full-scale Bulgarian rebellion was under way, with the various nationalist groups receiving support from Serbia, Montenegro and Russia. This crisis eventually escalated into a full-scale war between Russia and Turkey from 1877 to 1878 over the future of Bulgaria, culminating in defeat for the Ottoman Empire, which was forced to sign the Treaty of San Stefano (1878). Under this agreement, Bulgaria was given virtual independence, Serbia and Romania received territory and Russia and Austria-Hungary agreed to supervise reforms in Bosnia-Herzegovina. However, the British and Austro-Hungarian governments believed that the agreement had given Russia too much power in the Balkans. In the end, Bismarck decided to play 'honest broker' in the crisis, and proposed an international congress in Berlin. Under the Treaty of Berlin (1878), it was agreed that Russia would retain its territorial gains, Serbia, Montenegro and Romania would keep their independence, and Bosnia-Herzegovina would be placed under the exclusive administration of Austria-Hungary.

The settlement of Bulgaria's territory proved more sensitive, and less satisfactory. Bulgaria was turned into an autonomous principality of the Ottoman Empire, with a Christian government and a national army. However, major changes were proposed to its existing boundaries, with the aim of preserving Ottoman power: south and south-west Bulgaria (dubbed 'Big Bulgaria') and Eastern Rumelia were allowed to remain under Ottoman rule. This served to encourage more civil unrest. In 1885, nationalists in Eastern Rumelia revolted against Ottoman rule and demanded the right to join the rest of Bulgaria. The Russian government used the revolt as a pretext to gain further territory. However, Austria-Hungary wanted Bulgaria to remain completely

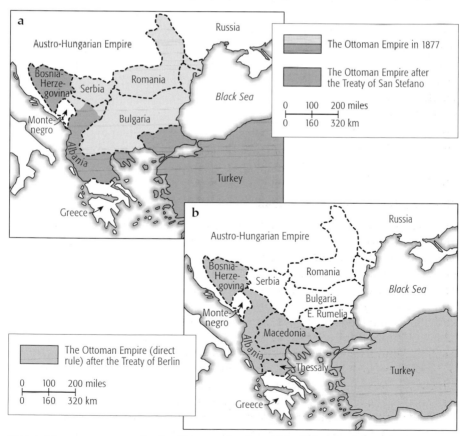

Map 1. The consequences for the Ottoman Empire and for Bulgaria of the Bulgarian Crisis, 1878: (a) after the Treaty of San Stefano and (b) after the Treaty of Berlin.

ıdent of tsarist influence and enlisted the support of Bismarck, who
ith the Habsburg monarchy (which presided over the Austro-Hungarian
Empire), much to the annoyance of the Tsar, who was forced to withdraw
Russian troops from Bulgaria, which remained independent.

The Bulgarian Crisis revealed the complexity of the Balkan problem, which
revolved around nationalist demands for self-determination, the gradual
decline of Ottoman rule and the designs of Russia and Austria-Hungary.
It showed how easily problems in the Balkans could create a delicate
international situation. More importantly, the crisis revealed that in any
Habsburg–tsarist dispute, Germany was not prepared to see Russia profit.
The significance of the Bulgarian Crisis was threefold: it put an end to the
League of the Three Emperors; it severely weakened Germany's role as a
so-called 'honest broker' in the Balkans; and it killed the Re-Insurance Treaty,
which the Russians saw as a worthless and unscrupulous agreement that was
not renewed.

Thus, even the shrewd diplomacy of Bismarck foundered on the rocks of
the Balkans. The attempt to balance the irreconcilable differences between
Austria-Hungary and Russia was really an exercise in crisis management
rather than a real solution to the conflict between the two powers in the region.
Even so, Bismarck's fall from power in 1890 is still viewed as a key turning
point on the road to war. After all, the German leaders who followed him
favoured confrontation over conciliation. Obviously, Bismarck's cautious policy
was successful in the short term, but there is no guarantee that he would have
continued to adopt such a conciliatory line had he remained in office. He was
already coming under increasing pressure to adopt a popular aggressive and
expansionist foreign policy before his abrupt dismissal by the young Kaiser
Wilhelm II. Paradoxically, the fact that Bismarck's alliance diplomacy had
placed Germany in such a strong diplomatic position actually encouraged
other, less shrewd German figures in the aristocracy, army and navy to push
for a bolder and more expansionist foreign policy.[5]

The impact of imperialism

It was not only the swift rise of Germany which created a climate of tension
in European affairs. Another development was to have an equally profound
impact: the sudden and unexpected upsurge of imperialism from 1880 to 1914
in Africa and Asia. The governments of Britain, France, Germany and Italy, and
King Leopold II of the Belgians, all became entangled in a rapid partition of
Africa, which resulted in 90 per cent of all African territory being brought
under European rule. Russia, Britain, France, Japan, Germany and the USA all
took part in a similarly feverish scramble for territorial gains in Asia. The major
European powers saw this 'new imperialism' as a battle for wealth, growth,
power and survival.[6] Lord Salisbury, the British prime minister, said that the
world was being divided into 'living and dying' powers.[7] To remain a great
power, or to become one, seemed to require the possession of an empire.

The causes of this amazing search for territory are extremely complex. Local traders, agents, bankers and investors encouraged imperial expansion and expected European governments to defend their interests. This produced a number of diverse responses. Bondholders pressed the British government to occupy Egypt in 1882; Karl Peters, a German explorer, called on Bismarck to help consolidate the gains of his German East Africa Company; George Goldie asked the British government for help to consolidate his palm-oil monopoly on the Niger river; owners of gold mines and diamond mines pressed the British government to defend their interests in South Africa; and major industrial companies attempted to gain a monopoly over supplies of raw materials in Africa and Asia. In many cases, a number of local difficulties often dragged reluctant governments in to defend national interests. Local nationalist movements also played their part: some sought to defend territory in Africa and Asia, others wanted to collaborate with specific European powers in order to retain some semblance of local influence.

The motive of each of the European powers is likewise complex. The British government wished to maintain its dominance in the colonial sphere; as other European powers sought to expand, the British responded by seizing colonies. The French saw its empire partly in terms of economic gain and partly in terms of helping to restore its damaged national pride after its defeat by Germany in the Franco-Prussian War. King Leopold II of Belgium sought an empire to enhance his own status and for purely economic reward. The Italians coveted territory to emphasise their claims to be treated as a major European power. The German government often used imperialism to increase its popularity at home.

A principal aim of all the European powers was to gain territory by attacking small, weak powers and pre-industrial peoples, and to ensure that such conflicts remained localised. Where any discord over territory arose, European powers often co-operated in diplomatic agreements to make sure that such crises did not escalate. The partition of West Africa, for example, was decided peacefully by a number of European powers at the West Africa Conference in Berlin (1884–85). Britain and Germany settled their problems in East Africa by peaceful negotiation. The European scramble for trading rights in China was also resolved by diplomatic agreement. On the other hand, imperial problems served to intensify the rivalry between many European powers: Anglo-French differences in North Africa almost ended in war at Fashoda in 1898, while Anglo-Russian relations often reached the point of war over issues of mutual interest in Persia, Afghanistan and China. The relations of Japan and Russia deteriorated over their imperial differences in Asia, and actually did result in war between 1904 and 1905, which resulted in a surprise Japanese victory.

The most unfortunate consequences of the 'new imperialism' were the creation of an atmosphere of heightened patriotism (known as jingoism), the glorification of armed force, and the denial of national self-determination to small powers. Major European powers became obsessed with gaining further territory and showing no sign of weakness. The principle of the large powers grabbing territory from the small powers, a key aspect of the 'new imperialism', caused tension. It is probably correct to suggest that the First World War was not directly caused by the 'new imperialism', but that its influence on future events was not insignificant. The craving of the great powers to expand at the expense of weaker states, and the hunger of the weaker states, especially in eastern Europe, for self-determination, created an atmosphere in which mutual antagonism became the order of the day. British fears of imperial decline, German ambitions for an empire, and Austro-Hungarian anxiety regarding a loss of its power, were all linked to the general 'survival-of-the-fittest' mood which the imperialist age had profoundly influenced. The imperialist idea of struggle and rivalry emphasised the need for bold new policies and dynamic solutions to problems in international relations.

Kaiser Wilhelm, German world policy and German aims

The desire for a bold new approach to foreign policy was most noticeable in Germany. In 1897, Kaiser Wilhelm II announced that Germany would adopt a 'world policy' (*Weltpolitik*). The logic behind *Weltpolitik* seemed reasonable enough: the Kaiser claimed that German industrial expansion was so dependent on imports of raw materials from overseas that a vast colonial empire was required, with a large navy to support it. Thus, *Weltpolitik* was committed to a large programme of naval expansion and heavy involvement in colonial affairs. However, this abrupt change in German policy, from the prudence of Bismarck to the confrontational style of Kaiser Wilhelm, marks a crucial turning point in Germany's foreign policy in the years which led to war.[8] The reasons why Kaiser Wilhelm opted for *Weltpolitik* have been the subject of enormous debate. The timing of the policy is usually put down to the appointment by the Kaiser of von Bülow as chancellor, and Admiral von Tirpitz as naval minister, who both favoured an expansionist foreign policy with three key aims.

1 To build a German navy which would match the best in the world. It was hoped that a strong German navy would encourage Britain to opt for neutrality in any future European war.
2 To make Germany a major imperial power. This implied territorial expansion overseas.
3 To use foreign-policy issues to increase support for authoritarian rule. This would weaken the appeal of socialism and democracy.

The real problem was that the Kaiser, the chancellor and leading foreign, military and naval advisers appeared to pursue perhaps one, but never all of these aims at any one time. The result was a lack of co-ordination in foreign policy, and a great deal of confusion over whether *Weltpolitik* was a genuine attempt to find Germany 'a place in the sun' or whether it was merely a useful political tactic to weaken the domestic appeal of social democracy at home.

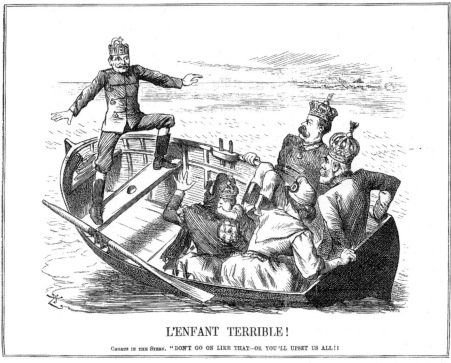

L'ENFANT TERRIBLE !

Chorus in the Stern. "DON'T GO ON LIKE THAT—OR YOU'LL UPSET US ALL!!

A *Punch* cartoon of 1890 shows the new Kaiser with representatives of Russia, Britain, France and Austria-Hungary. What point is the cartoonist trying to make?

The rhetoric used by German leaders in pursuit of *Weltpolitik* was often daring and confrontational. The German government engaged in a clear orchestration of patriotism. The German press, heavily influenced by the Kaiser's press office, whipped up jingoism and fomented antagonism against other nations. Nationalist pressure groups, including the Navy League, the Colonial Society and the Pan-German League, supported *Weltpolitik*. German history books venerated great German conquests of the past. The Kaiser often saw *Weltpolitik* as a means of warding off the rise of socialism in Germany by diverting attention towards external issues. Admiral von Tirpitz, the prime mover in building the German navy, was fully aware that a naval race could act as a rallying point for German public opinion in support of the existing authoritarian government. The success or failure of *Weltpolitik* therefore became a central issue in German domestic politics.[9]

The policy created a great deal of tension, accomplished very little, and soured international relations. In the view of Bethmann Hollweg, the German chancellor who replaced von Bülow, *Weltpolitik* had 'challenged everybody, got in everybody's way but actually weakened nobody'. The Kaiser never contemplated the conflict that a bold, expansionist Germany foreign policy would provoke abroad. The major world powers had no intention of smoothing the path for Germany to become a dominant world power and Germany met hostility in every direction. The British engaged in a naval race and maintained supremacy. The USA thwarted German ambitions in Venezuela and the Philippines, the British and French obstructed German ambitions in Morocco, and the British and French denied Germany capital to build the Berlin–Baghdad Railway. All the major European powers ganged up together to ensure that Germany made no significant economic gains in China in 1900. The only territorial gains that Germany made in its search for *Weltpolitik* were small gains in the Congo, a 99-year lease on Kiao-chow in China, two small Samoan islands, some small Pacific islands and a fleet of costly dreadnought battleships, which were not used in battle during the First World War, except at the Battle of Jutland. *Weltpolitik* is a classic case of ambition outweighing common sense. The German government wasted a great deal of effort in pursuing a policy which was both costly and led other European powers to regard Germany as a real danger to European peace.

The drift towards alliances

The most unfortunate consequence of *Weltpolitik* was the impact which it had on European diplomatic alignments. In 1871, there was no system of fixed military alliances among the major European powers. The creation of peacetime alliances began with Bismarck's Dual Alliance (1879) and Triple Alliance (1882). Both agreements were seen as defensive, and produced no rival set of alliances. Yet German support for Austria-Hungary during the Bulgarian Crisis led to much friendlier Franco-Russian relations, which eventually resulted in the formation of a firm military alliance in 1894. Under the terms of the Franco-Russian Alliance, each power pledged military co-operation in the event of war against any member of the Triple Alliance. This created a second alliance grouping in Europe, with the clear aim of checking German ambitions. In direct consequence of this agreement, French investment poured into Russia to support the development of its industry and economy, and close diplomatic and military links grew.

These alliances also encouraged the development of detailed military plans. The German army had to plan for a war on two fronts. In 1905, for example, General von Schlieffen developed a detailed war plan that involved a quick and decisive attack on France, followed by an all-out assault on Russia. The Russian army chiefs also made detailed plans for a rapid assault on Austria-Hungary and East Prussia in the event of war. French military chiefs planned a lightning offensive against Germany on the latter's western front. Thus the idea of fighting a future war within a coalition was becoming firmly planted in Germany, Austria-Hungary and Italy, as well as in France and Russia.[10]

The only major European power outside these two alliance groups was Britain, which remained in 'splendid', but increasingly precarious, isolation. However, the hectic imperial rivalry of the late nineteenth century had extended British military and naval resources to breaking point. The emergence of Germany as a major colonial and naval rival caused deep concern. Russia was also a menace to British India. The growth of Japan in the Far East, and continuing Anglo-French rivalry in Africa and Indo-China, further fuelled the idea that Britain's military resources were becoming seriously over-stretched. Many prominent British statesmen started to call for an end to Britain's diplomatic isolation. In 1898, negotiations were started, intending to build an Anglo-German 'understanding', but animosity between Britain and Germany intensified during the era of *Weltpolitik*, largely over naval rivalry, and the idea was dropped.

The first move by the British government away from isolation was the signing of the Anglo-Japanese Treaty (1902), which was designed to ease Britain's worry over trade in the region and to ease fears over the Russian threat to India. However, the Anglo-Japanese Alliance encouraged Japan to go to war with Russia between 1904 and 1905, when it gained an unexpected victory. A more significant agreement was the Entente Cordiale, signed in 1904 between Britain and France. This cleared up Anglo-French colonial differences in Africa and Asia: the French agreed to British primacy in Egypt in return for a 'free hand' in Morocco. The Anglo-French entente was a colonial agreement, and gave no promise of military co-operation in the event of a European war. [11]

The Entente Cordiale was not viewed in this way by the Kaiser, however, who suspected that it was a secret military alliance aimed at 'encircling Germany'. He wanted to test the closeness of the agreement. In January 1905, a French diplomatic mission arrived in Fez to seek special privileges for French traders in Morocco. In March 1905, in a tense and provocative move, Kaiser Wilhelm steamed into the Moroccan port of Tangier aboard a German naval vessel, requested equal treatment for German trade, and offered German support to maintain Moroccan independence. In May 1905, Lord Lansdowne, the British foreign secretary, sent a message to the French government, which gave some vague hope that the entente might, under certain circumstances, be converted into a military alliance. Delcassé, the French foreign minister, interpreted this as an offer by Britain to enter into an Anglo-French alliance, which it clearly was not. The Kaiser insisted that the French government should dismiss Delcassé for seeking to sour Franco-German relations. In response, the French government, unprepared to face Germany in war, and with no promise of British support, sacked Delcassé and agreed to settle Franco-German differences over Morocco at an international conference. This decisive show of strength by the Kaiser had seemingly shown that the Entente Cordiale was little more than a worthless piece of paper.

The Algeciras Conference duly took place between January and April 1906. However, Sir Edward Grey, the new Liberal foreign secretary, expressed private concerns over the high-handed behaviour of the Kaiser during the Delcassé affair, and offered enthusiastic British support for French claims in Morocco. The Russian government, under prompting from France, offered similar encouragement. As a result, the French gained a significant diplomatic victory over Germany at Algeciras. Morocco's independence was confirmed, but France and Spain gained authority over the police, and France was given control over the Moroccan central bank.[12] All that the Kaiser's bullying had achieved was to heighten fears in France, Britain and Russia about German imperial ambitions. This simply encouraged the development of closer Franco-Russian relations and set British foreign policy in a clear, anti-German direction. In the wake of the crisis, Grey ordered Anglo-French military conversations and sought to improve Anglo-Russian relations. In 1907, Britain signed the Anglo-Russian Convention, which settled Anglo-Russian imperial differences in Afghanistan, Tibet and Persia (modern-day Iran).[13] The German government saw the agreement as a bitter blow which cemented its growing diplomatic encirclement. The term 'Triple Entente' (of France, Russia and Britain) started to be used to describe the new diplomatic friendship between these three major European powers.

The Anglo-German naval race, which reached its most excitable stage between 1908 and 1910, added to international tension. The German desire for a navy on a world scale met a British desire to maintain its naval supremacy. The speed at which new, state-of-the-art dreadnought-class battleships could be built in Britain and Germany produced panic and antagonism. The Anglo-German naval race soured British attitudes towards Germany more than any other factor. Sir Edward Grey claimed that it was the major reason why Britain went to war in 1914.[14] From 1907 to 1914, British naval expenditure increased from £31.5 to £50 million per annum in order to meet the German challenge and to maintain supremacy. Robert Cecil, a Conservative MP, claimed that as the Germans wanted a large fleet and the British were determined to maintain supremacy, there was 'no hope of finding common ground'.[15] The Anglo-German naval race led the British government to become even more disturbed and frightened about the direction of German policy.

The 1908-09 Bosnian Crisis served to stir up Russian fears about German aims in the Balkans. In October 1908, Austria-Hungary suddenly annexed Bosnia-Herzegovina as a result of its fear of a spread of the 'Young Turk' (a reforming movement active in the Ottoman Empire) revolution. The Tsar expressed outrage at the annexation, but the Kaiser said that if Russia went to war over the issue, Germany would stand by Austria-Hungary. *The Times* claimed that the Kaiser had stood by Austria in 'shining armour'. This dose of German diplomatic bullying made the Russian government all the more resolved to increase its defence expenditure, draw closer to its potential allies, and not back down in the Balkans again.[16]

In 1911, a second major crisis over Morocco brought Europe to the very edge of war. In May 1911, the French government sent troops to put down a revolt in Fez. In July, a German gunboat arrived in the Moroccan port of Agadir in a provocative move designed to gain colonial concessions from France. Sir Edward Grey offered the French government full support throughout the Agadir Crisis. In October 1911, the German government decided to seek a negotiated settlement of the crisis, and received territory in the Congo in return for recognising French control in Morocco.[17] The Agadir Crisis brought a danger of war, and drew Britain and France closer together in the face of the German threat. *Weltpolitik* was revealed as a dangerous and provocative policy. After Agadir, the British made a firm plan to send a British Expeditionary Force (BEF) of 150,000 troops to France in the event of war, and signed naval agreements with both France and Russia.

During these years, the military and diplomatic balance of power in Europe was turning sharply against Germany, which had only one firm European ally – Austria-Hungary – and one unreliable ally – Italy. The military situation was even more dismal: in 1912, the German army numbered 761,000 and the Austro-Hungarian army was 450,000 strong. Against this stood the Russian army of 1.3 million, the French army of 600,000 and the British Expeditionary Force of 150,000.[18] The naval situation was even more worrying. A great deal of German money had been used to build dreadnoughts, but the British had maintained a clear naval supremacy and, with the support of Russia and France, could clearly mount an effective blockade against Germany. In these gloomy circumstances, the German press talked of Germany being 'encircled by a hostile coalition of envious powers', while leading military figures urged a 'preventative war' to break Germany free from its diplomatic isolation. The whole trend of European diplomacy was leading in the direction of two power blocs which were likely, sooner or later, to go to war with one another. In 1912, German military leaders, once so proud and confident, now grew increasingly pessimistic about how sharply the balance of power was moving against them.

The Balkan Crisis, 1912–14

From 1912 to 1914, the major focus of European attention switched to the Balkans. This area was a labyrinth of ethnic tensions, nationalist groups and great power rivalry. The most immediate problem was the growth of nationalist groups determined to break free of Ottoman rule. Most European powers worried most about which power would profit from the death of the 'sick man of Europe' – the Ottoman Empire. In 1897, Russia and Austria-Hungary had signed an agreement which 'put the Balkans on ice'. However, both powers remained deeply interested in the power balance in the region, and would not remain indifferent for long. Of the remaining Balkan powers, Romania, Greece and Montenegro were independent, though the Turks still had influence over Macedonia and Albania. Turkey itself was in a state of turmoil: the 'Young Turk' movement had revolted in 1908 and demanded liberal reforms. This alarmed the Habsburg monarchy, which annexed Bosnia-Herzegovina, thereby arousing festering Russian anger. In the same year, Bulgaria renounced Turkish rule.

The final character in this Balkan inferno was Serbia, a vibrant, independent power. In 1903, King Alexander was assassinated – along with his wife. This brought King Peter, of the pro-Russian Karadjordjevic dynasty, to power, who was hostile towards the Ottoman and Habsburg empires and equally resolved to build a strong Balkan confederation to free all Slavs from alien rule. He looked to tsarist Russia for assistance in this enterprise and, in 1903, a firm

Russo-Serb military alliance was signed. However, the Habsburg monarchy saw Serbia as a major nuisance in the Balkans and was determined to thwart its territorial ambitions. The annexation of Bosnia-Herzegovina in 1908 was a prime example of this desire. It quite blatantly provoked Serb resentment and encouraged the tsarist government to draw closer to Serbia.

After 1908, Serbia made a daring bid to create a Balkan coalition. The outcome of a hectic period of Serbian diplomatic activity was the formation of the Balkan League (1912), which consisted of Serbia, Bulgaria, Greece and Montenegro. The chief aim of this Pan-Slavic coalition was to force the Turks out of the Balkans. The weakness of the Turks was already evident, given the success that the Italian army had enjoyed in Libya during 1911. In October 1912, the Balkan League seized its opportunity and declared war on Turkey (the First Balkan War) and gained a swift victory which drove the Turks out of most of the European territory of the Balkans.

Surprisingly, the major European powers kept out of the fighting, but took a sharp interest in the negotiations for a peace settlement. These were held in London, under the chairmanship of Sir Edward Grey. Bitter disagreements between the members of the Balkan League over the division of territory quickly came to the surface. It took a full six months of bitter argument, interspersed with further fighting, before the Treaty of London (1913), which

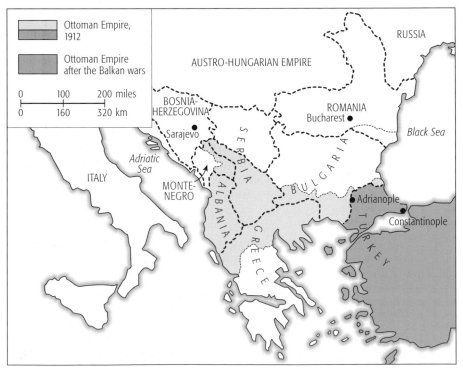

Map 2. The outcome of the Balkan wars, 1912–13 (for the extent of the territory of Macedonia, divided mainly between Serbia and Greece, see Map 1b).

settled the First Balkan War, was eventually signed. The London agreement gave Serbia, Bulgaria and Greece nearly all the European territory of the Ottoman Empire, except Albania. This enraged Serbia as this was its key territorial objective, because it would have given Serbia an Adriatic port, which, for a land-locked country, was seen as vital for its future economic development. The Greek government also felt cheated, as Greece did not gain a larger share of territory in Macedonia and Bulgaria. The Bulgarian government thought that Bulgaria had gained very little at all. The volatile Balkan coalition soon fell apart.

A second Balkan War broke out in June 1913, when Bulgaria attacked Serbia. This prompted Greece, Romania and Turkey all to declare war on Bulgaria. In less than a month, Bulgaria had been quite easily defeated. The Treaty of Bucharest (1913) forced the Bulgarians to give Serbia large gains in Macedonia, but under Austrian and German pressure the Serbs were once again denied an Adriatic port. The Treaty of Constantinople (1913) allowed Turkey to gain Adrianople and other territory lost to Bulgaria during the first Balkan conflict.[19]

The Balkan Wars ruined the dream of a Pan-Slav coalition, but they ended with the Ottoman Empire having been virtually driven out of its European territory. Equally, Bulgaria was isolated and severely weakened, and the power of Greece and Serbia had greatly increased.[20] The outcome of the Balkan Wars was really a body-blow to the strategic position of Austria-Hungary. Serbia, with the alliance of Russia and an army 200,000 strong, and with 200,000 reservists, was a clear threat to Bosnia-Herzegovina. The Austro-Hungarian government now depended on Germany for its survival as a major power in the Balkans.[21]

1914: the July Crisis and decisions for war

In the summer of 1914, Archduke Franz Ferdinand, nephew of Franz Josef I, the Austrian emperor, and heir to the Habsburg throne, decided to visit Sarajevo, the capital of Bosnia. Sarajevo was a very dangerous place for a member of the Habsburg royal family to visit, because it was a citadel of Serb and Bosnian nationalist groups. The date chosen for the visit was of great emotional significance for Serb nationalists as it marked the anniversary of a famous victory by the Turks over the Serbs at the Battle of Kosovo in the fourteenth century. Austrian diplomats warned the archduke of the dangers that he faced, but Franz Ferdinand, headstrong, and a harsh opponent of Slav nationalism, ignored the warning. On the pleasant morning of 28 June 1914, Franz Ferdinand arrived in Sarajevo and paraded through the streets in an open-topped car, accompanied by his spouse. At 11.30 a.m. the car moved slowly past a large group of young people lining the route. A demonstration broke out. The car stopped. A young man, who had waited for hours, then rushed from the crowd and shot the archduke and his wife dead. The assassin was Gavrilo Princip, a teenage rebel whose cause was 'Young Bosnia', a nationalist group which aimed to drive the Habsburgs out of Bosnia. His gun was given to him by a pro-Serb group known as the 'Black Hand'.[22] By pulling the trigger of that gun, this unknown Bosnian teenager set off a chain of events which ultimately led to the outbreak of the First World War.

The news of the death of Archduke Franz Ferdinand produced fury in Austria. The Austrian government immediately decided to pin the blame for the assassination on the Serbian government, even though they had no proof of this. Count von Berchtold, the Austrian foreign minister, advised Franz Josef to use the assassination as a pretext to 'settle accounts' with Serbia. On 4 July 1914, Franz Josef sent a letter to Kaiser Wilhelm asking for German support to 'eliminate Serbia as a power factor in the Balkans'.[23] The Kaiser consulted with Bethmann Hollweg, the German chancellor, to decide the German position. They agreed that Austria should be given a free hand (known as the 'blank cheque') to start war with Serbia. Of course, they hoped that a war between Austria-Hungary and Serbia would remain localised, but both knew that the crisis might bring Russian intervention, and a European war. The German government was prepared to risk this, in order to secure a victory for Austria-Hungary over Serbia.[24] The Kaiser advised the Austrian government that Austria-Hungary 'must judge what is to be done to clear up her relations with Serbia; but whatever Austria's decision, she could count with certainty upon it, that Germany would stand behind her'.[25] The German reply was exactly what the Austrian government had wanted. It was decided to issue an ultimatum to the Serbian government, framed in a manner that would be likely to provoke war.

The Russian and French governments met from 20 July to 23 July 1914 to discuss their positions in view of the escalating crisis. Poincaré, the French president, gave his full support to Russia in resisting any attempt by Austria-Hungary to threaten the independence of Serbia. This is viewed as a second 'blank cheque', which encouraged the Russian government to risk a war with Germany and Austria-Hungary. However, the French government advised Russia to do nothing during the July Crisis that would be likely to provoke Germany. Equally, the Russian government sought a negotiated settlement to the crisis. The Tsar begged the Kaiser to restrain Austria-Hungary, without success, throughout the crisis. The French decision to support Russia was designed to deter Austria-Hungary, but the German decision to support Austria-Hungary aimed to provoke. This is the fundamental difference between the two so-called 'blank cheques' issued during the July Crisis.[26]

The crisis escalated on 23 July 1914, when the Austrian government finally delivered its ultimatum to Serbia. The ultimatum claimed that Serbia was involved in the assassination of the archduke, and made ten demands designed to put down the terrorist activities of Serb nationalists, including joint Habsburg–Serb action to suppress all movements opposed to the Dual Monarchy (Austria-Hungary) in Serbia. It was assumed by most European governments that Serbia would reject the ultimatum. The Russian government advised Serbia to take a conciliatory and co-operative line. The Serbian government followed this advice, and agreed to most of Austria's demands, but insisted that any investigation of the problem should adhere to international law.[27] However, the Austro-Hungarian government claimed that it would only accept immediate Serbian acceptance of the original ultimatum. Sir Edward Grey proposed a conference in London to work out a peaceful settlement, but this was rejected by Austria-Hungary and Germany. The Tsar told the Serbian government that he wanted a peaceful solution, but would not remain 'indifferent to the fate of Serbia'. It seems that the German government desired the conflict to remain localised, but made no effort to restrain the Austrian government, or to put pressure upon it to accept a negotiated settlement.

The first declaration of war in the crisis came on 28 July 1914, when Austria-Hungary declared war on Serbia. However, the hope of both Austria-Hungary and Germany that such a war could remained localised proved illusory.[28] The Russian government made it very clear that Russia would go to war to save Serbia unless Austria-Hungary withdrew its troops from Serbian territory. The Austro-Hungarian government refused. On 29 July 1914, the Russian government announced that it had no alternative but to make plans for the mobilisation of its troops, though it still wished for a negotiated settlement.[29]

The German government informed the Tsar that Russian mobilisation would lead to German mobilisation. Bethmann Hollweg made a last-minute plea for British neutrality in the event of war,[30] but the British government refused to give any such soothing assurance. As usual, the British would 'wait on events'. The main contribution of the British government to the July Crisis was to make a number of proposals to Serbia, Austria-Hungary, Germany and Russia to settle the matter by negotiation, which were rejected by the German and Austro-Hungarian governments.[31]

On 30 July 1914, the Tsar announced that Russian mobilisation would take place on the following day. The German timetable for war now swung into rapid action. Von Moltke, the German military chief of staff, told the Kaiser that German military planning was based on swift action: the Schlieffen Plan involved a speedy attack on France, via Belgium, followed by a move eastwards to face Russia. The urgency Germany felt to implement the Schlieffen Plan now dominated events.[32] In the final analysis, the German government cannot be accused of cold-bloodedly planning a European war. However, Germany can be accused of not making a serious effort to persuade Austria-Hungary to withdraw its ultimatum, or to bring about a peaceful settlement. The last-minute plea by the Kaiser for the Austro-Hungarian army to accept negotiations once they had occupied Belgrade was fairly half-hearted. Equally, the passionate German desire to implement the Schlieffen Plan required an escalation of the crisis from a Balkan dispute into a European war.

On 31 July 1914, the German government sent the Russian government an ultimatum which said that unless Russia ceased all military preparations, Germany would have to declare war. In response, the Russian government claimed that its mobilisation plans inferred no aggressive action, and continued to express a desire for a peaceful settlement. Even so, on 1 August 1914, Germany declared war on Russia. On 2 August 1914, the German government sent an ultimatum to the Belgian government asking for permission to allow the German army safe passage for its now inevitable attack on France. It was over the issue of Belgian neutrality, to which Britain was committed, that the British government decided to act. Sir Edward Grey informed the German government that any breach of that neutrality would result in a British declaration of war.

On 3 August 1914, the German army invaded Belgium. A few hours later, Germany declared war on France, even though the French had no major interests in the Balkans. France became the victim of what seemed to be unprovoked aggression. The Italian government, which had been ignored by Germany and Austria-Hungary during the crisis, decided to remain neutral. On 4 August 1914, the British government finally declared war on Germany over the issue of Belgian neutrality. Even so, Sir Edward Grey had long realised that Britain could not afford to stand aside and see France crushed by Germany. The First World War, which most of the participants believed would be over quickly, lasted for four savage and bloody years.

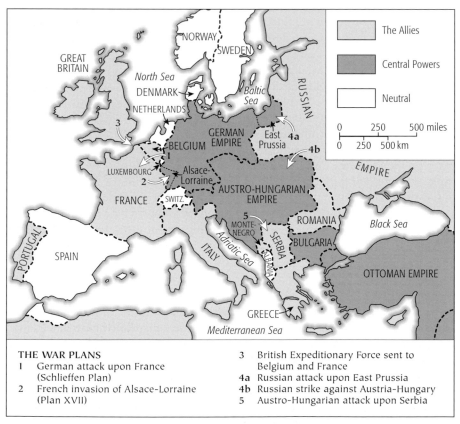

THE WAR PLANS

1 German attack upon France (Schlieffen Plan)
2 French invasion of Alsace-Lorraine (Plan XVII)
3 British Expeditionary Force sent to Belgium and France
4a Russian attack upon East Prussia
4b Russian strike against Austria-Hungary
5 Austro-Hungarian attack upon Serbia

Map 3. The war plans of the European powers, 1914.

The July Crisis of 1914

1.1 The German 'blank cheque' to Austria

Count Szogyney, Austrian ambassador in Berlin to Count Leopold Berchtold, Austro-Hungarian foreign minister, 5 July 1914 (letter)

After lunch, when I again called attention to the seriousness of the situation, the Kaiser authorised me to inform our gracious Majesty that we might in this case, as in all others, rely upon Germany's full support. He must first hear what the Imperial Chancellor [Bethmann Hollweg] has to say, but he did not doubt in the least that Herr von Bethmann Hollweg would agree with him. Especially as far as our action against Serbia was concerned. But it was his [Kaiser Wilhelm's] opinion that this action must not be delayed. Russia's attitude will no doubt be hostile, but to this he had been for years prepared, and should a war between Austria-Hungary be unavoidable, we might be convinced that Germany, our faithful ally, would stand by our side. Russia at the present time was in no way prepared for war, and would think twice before it appealed to arms. But it will certainly set other powers on the Triple Alliance and add fuel to the fire in the Balkans. He understands perfectly well that His Apostolic Majesty [the emperor of Austria-Hungary] in his well-known love of peace would be reluctant to march into Serbia; but if we had really recognised the necessity of warlike action against Serbia, he [Kaiser Wilhelm] would regret if we did not make use of the present moment, which is all in our favour.

Source: I. Geiss (ed.), *July 1914*, London, 1967, pp. 76–77

1.2 Bethmann Hollweg on the Serb danger

Bethmann Hollweg, German chancellor to German ambassadors in Paris, London and St Petersburg, 21 July 1914 (letter)

The Serbian mischief-making goes back over a long number of years. The Greater Serbia chauvinism appeared in particularly marked form during the Bosnian Crisis. Only the extreme moderation and self-control of the Austro-Hungarian government and the energetic intervention of the great powers can be credited with the fact that the provocation to which Austria-Hungary was at that time exposed did not lead to war. The Serbian government has not made good its assurances of future good conduct which it made at that time. The Greater Serbia propaganda has since been continually increasing in extent and intensity under the very eyes of official Serbia, and, at least, with tacit consent. It is to the account of that propaganda that the latest outrage [the assassination of Archduke Franz Ferdinand and his wife], the trail of which leads to Belgrade, can be charged. It has become unmistakably evident that it would no longer comport, either with the dignity or the self-preservation of the Austro-Hungarian monarchy, to regard inactively any longer the mischief-making on the other side of the border – mischief-making by which the security and integrity of its dominions are lastingly menaced. In such a state of affairs, neither the procedure nor the demands of the Austro-Hungarian government can be regarded as otherwise than moderate and proper.

Source: I. Geiss (ed.), *July 1914*, London, 1967, pp. 149–50

1.3 The British attitude to the crisis

Sir Edward Grey, foreign secretary, to George Buchanan, British ambassador to St Petersburg, Russia, 25 July 1914 (letter)

I gave no indication that we would stand aside; on the contrary, I said to the German ambassador that, as long as there was only a dispute between Austria and Serbia alone, I did not feel entitled to intervene, but that, directly it was a matter between Austria and Russia, it became a question of the peace of Europe, which concerned us all. I had furthermore spoken on the assumption that Russia would mobilise, whereas the assumption of the German government had hitherto been, officially, that Serbia would receive no support, and what I said must influence the German government to take the matter seriously.

Source: G. P. Gooch and H. Temperley (eds.), *British documents on the outbreak of war, 1898–1914*, document no. 132, 11 vols., London, 1926–38

1.4 Tsar Nicholas appeals to the Kaiser

Nicholas II to Wilhelm II, 29 July 1914 (telegram)

In this serious moment I appeal to you to help me. An ignoble war has been declared on a weak country [Serbia]. The indignation in Russia, fully shared by me, is enormous. I foresee that very soon I shall be overwhelmed by the pressure brought upon me, and be forced to take measures which will lead to war. To try and avoid such a calamity as a European war, I beg you in the name of our old friendship to do what you can to stop your allies going too far.

Source: I. Geiss (ed.), *July 1914*, London, 1967, pp. 260–61

1.5 A German military summary of the crisis

Count Helmuth von Moltke, German chief of military staff, to Bethmann Hollweg, 29 July 1914 (memorandum)

For more than five years Serbia has been a cause of a European tension, which has been pressing with simply intolerable weight on the political and economic existence of nations. With a patience approaching weakness, Austria has up to the present borne the continuous provocation and the political machinations aimed at the disruption of her own national stability which proceeded by regicide at home to the murder of princes in a neighbouring land. It was only after the last despicable crime that she took too extreme measures, in order to burn out with a glowing iron a cancer that has constantly threatened to poison the body of Europe . . . All Europe would have drawn a breath of relief if this mischief-maker could have been properly chastised and peace and order thus restored to the Balkans, but Russia placed herself at the side of the criminal nation . . . The Austro-Serbian affair is a purely private quarrel in which, as has been said, nobody in Europe would have a profound interest and which would in no way threaten the peace of Europe, but would establish it more firmly, if Russia had not interfered with it . . . If Austria advances into Serbia she will have to face not only the Serbian army, but also the vast superior strength of Russia . . . At the moment, however, in which Austria mobilises her whole army, the collision between herself and Russia will become inevitable. But that, for Germany, is the cause of war. If Germany is not false to her word and permits her ally to suffer annihilation at the hands of Russian superiority, she too must mobilise . . . the mutual butchery of the civilised nations of Europe will begin . . . Germany does not want to bring this frightful war. But the German government knows that it would be violating in ominous fashion the deep-rooted feelings of fidelity which are among the most beautiful traits of the German character and would be setting itself against the sentiments of the nation, if it did not come to the assistance of an ally.

Source: I. Geiss (ed.), *July 1914*, London, 1967, pp. 283–84

1.6 Bethmann Hollweg pleads for Britain to remain neutral

Sir Edward Goschen, British ambassador in Berlin, to Sir Edward Grey, 29 July 1914 (telegram)

Bethmann Hollweg, chancellor, having just returned from Potsdam sent for me again tonight and made the following strong bid for British neutrality in the event of war. He said he was continuing his efforts to maintain peace, but that in the event of a Russian attack on Austria, Germany's obligation as Austria's ally might, to his great regret, render a European conflagration inevitable, and in that case hoped Britain would remain neutral. As far as he was able to judge the keynote of British policy, it was evident that Great Britain would not allow France to be crushed. Such a result was not contemplated by Germany. The imperial government was ready to give every assurance to the British government provided that Britain remained neutral.

Source: G. P. Gooch and H. Temperley (eds.), *British documents on the outbreak of war, 1898–1914*, document no. 305, 11 vols., London, 1926–38

1.7 Sir Edward Grey refuses to promise Germany a pledge of British neutrality

Sir Edward Grey to Sir Edward Goschen, British ambassador in Berlin, 30 July 1914 (telegram)

You must inform the German chancellor that his proposal that we should bind ourselves to neutrality on such terms cannot for a moment be entertained . . . From the material point of view such a proposal is unacceptable, for France could be so crushed as to lose her position as a great power and become subordinate to German policy without further territory in Europe being taken from her . . . But apart from that for us to make a bargain with Germany at the expense of France would be a disgrace from which the good name of this country would never recover . . . The chancellor also asks us to bargain away whatever obligations or interest we have as regards the neutrality of Belgium. We could not entertain that bargain either . . . You should add most earnestly that the one way of maintaining the good relations between England and Germany is to continue to work together to preserve the peace of Europe.

Source: G. P. Gooch and H. Temperley (eds.), *British documents on the outbreak of war, 1898–1914*, document no. 303, 11 vols., London, 1926–38

Document case-study questions

1 What conclusions can be made about the attitude of Kaiser Wilhelm II towards Austria as expressed in 1.1?

2 Comment on the significance of Bethmann Hollweg's views on Serbia in 1.2.

3 Is it possible to identify the position of Grey towards the July Crisis from 1.3?

4 How much significance would you attach to the views expressed by Tsar Nicholas in 1.4?

5 Offer a critical evaluation of the views expressed in 1.5.

6 Assess the strengths or weaknesses of 1.6 as a historical source.

7 What conclusions about British policy towards Germany can be drawn from 1.7?

8 Using all the sources, offer an explanation as to who you think was responsible for the outbreak of the First World War.

Notes and references

1 Of the numerous introductory studies of the origins of the First World War, the following are extremely useful: R. Henig, *The origins of the First World War*, London, 1989; J. Joll, *The origins of the First World War*, London, 1984; D. E. Lee, *The outbreak of the First World War: who was responsible?*, London, 1963; G. Martel, *The origins of the First World War*, London, 1987; A. J. P. Taylor, *The struggle for mastery in Europe*, London, 1954; A. J. P. Taylor, *War by timetable: how the First World War began*, London, 1969; and L. F. C. Turner, *Origins of the First World War*, London, 1970.

2 For the impact of Germany on Europe, see F. Fischer, *War of illusions*, London, 1975; W. O. Henderson, *The rise of German industrial power, 1834–1914*, Berkeley, 1972; P. M. Kennedy, *The rise and fall of the great powers: economic change and military conflict*, London, 1988, pp. 269–82; and N. Stone, *Europe transformed, 1878–1919*, London, 1983, pp. 159–99.

3 For a useful discussion of Bismarck's diplomacy, see E. Eyck, *Bismarck and the German Empire*, London, 1968. See also I. Geiss, *German foreign policy, 1871–1914*, London, 1976; and W. Langer, *European alliances and alignments, 1871–90*, London, 1972.

4 For a detailed examination, see S. E. Crowe, *The Berlin Conference, 1884–86*, Westport, 1970.

5 For an assessment of Bismarck's legacy on European relations, see I. Geiss, 'Origins of the First World War', in H. W. Koch (ed.), *The origins of the First World War*, London, 1984.

6 For a stimulating and thought-provoking examination of the relationship between the 'new imperialism' and the origins of the First World War, see Joll, *Origins*, pp. 148–70.

7 Quoted in Kennedy, *Rise and fall*, p. 251.

8 For detailed examinations of *Weltpolitik*, see C. M. Andrew, '*Weltpolitik* and the reshaping of the Dual Alliance', *Journal of Contemporary History*, vol. 1 (1966); F. Fisher, 'World policy, world power and German war aims', in Koch (ed.), *Origins*; I. Geiss, 'The German version of imperialism: *Weltpolitik*', in G. Schöllgen (ed.), *Escape into war? The foreign policy of imperial Germany*, Oxford, 1990; and D. Kaiser, 'Germany and the origins of the First World War', *Journal of Modern History*, vol. 56 (1983).

9 For a discussion of the relationship between German domestic politics and foreign policy, see W. Mommsen, 'Domestic factors in German foreign policy before the First World War', *Central European History*, vol. 6 (1973).

10 See Kennedy, *Rise and fall*, pp. 321–30; Joll, *Origins*, pp. 34–57.

11 The most detailed study of the British move away from 'splendid isolation' is G. Monger, *The end of isolation: British foreign policy, 1900–7*, London, 1963.

12 The crisis is explained in full in E. N. Anderson, *The First Moroccan Crisis*, Chicago, 1930.

13 B. J. Williams, 'The strategic background to the Anglo-Russian Entente of August 1907', *Historical Journal*, vol. 9 (1966).

14 M. Howard, 'The Edwardian arms race', in D. Read (ed.), *Edwardian England*, London, 1982.

15 *House of Commons debates*, 29 March 1909, cols. 74–78.

16 D. W. Sweet, 'The Bosnian Crisis' in F. H. Hinsley (ed.), *British foreign policy under Sir Edward Grey*, Cambridge, 1967.

17 See I. C. Barlow, *The Agadir Crisis*, Durham, 1940.

18 See Kennedy, *Rise and fall*, p. 307.

19 The complicated diplomacy of the Balkan Wars is examined in Turner, *Origins*, pp. 27–60.

20 R. J. Crampton, 'The Balkans as a factor in German foreign policy', *The Slavonic and Eastern European Review, 1911–14*, vol. 55 (1977).

21 N. Stone, 'Moltke and Conrad: relations between the Austro-Hungarian and German general staffs, 1909–14', *Historical Journal*, vol. 9 (1966).

22 The planning of the assassination at Sarajevo has been the subject of enormous research. It seems that a group of renegade Serbian officers led by Colonel Dragutin Dimitrievitch, head of Serbian military intelligence and leader of the 'Black Hand', provided the weapons and training to the 17 young Bosnians involved in the conspiracy. The Serbian government was investigating rumours of Serbian involvement in supplying arms to Bosnian nationalists at the time of the assassination. However, no evidence of official involvement by the Serbian government has ever been found.

23 A. J. P. Taylor, 'The outbreak of war', in Lee, *The outbreak*, p. 58.

24 See K. Jarausch, 'The illusion of limited war: Chancellor Bethmann Hollweg's calculated risk, July 1914', *Central European History*, vol. 2 (1969).

25 Quoted in Taylor, 'The outbreak', p. 58.

26 For Russian policy during the July Crisis, see K. Neilson, 'Russia', in K. M. Wilson (ed.), *Decisions for war, 1914*, London, 1995. For French policy, see J. V. Keiger, 'France' in the same volume.

27 For Serbia's role, see M. Cornwell, 'Serbia', in Wilson, *Decisions*.

28 For Austria-Hungary's role, see N. Stone, 'Hungary and the crisis of 1914', *Journal of Contemporary History*, vol. 1 (1966).

29 The impact of Russian mobilisation on the crisis is explored in L. F. C. Turner, 'The Russian mobilisation in 1914', *Journal of Contemporary History*, vol. 3 (1968).

30 For a detailed discussion of Bethmann Hollweg's behaviour during the July Crisis, see D. Kaiser, 'Germany and the origins of the First World War', *Journal of Modern History*, vol. 55 (1983).

31 For British policy during the July Crisis, see H. Butterfield, 'Sir Edward Grey in July 1914', *Irish Historical Studies*, vol. 14 (1965–66); and Z. Steiner, *Britain and the origins of the First World War*, London, 1977.

32 The effect of the war plans is examined fully in P. M. Kennedy, *The war plans of the great powers*, London, 1979.

2 The historians and the origins of the First World War

War guilt: the changing debate

The outbreak of the First World War is one of the most controversial and repeatedly debated subjects in history.[1] The historical debate has been intensely affected by the prevailing political climate and by the urge to find out who was primarily responsible. This quest for a guilty party began almost as soon as the first shots were fired. The official report on the origins of the First World War, written by the victorious powers, and presented to the Versailles Peace Conference in 1919, offered two conclusions:

1 The war was premeditated by Germany and its allies and resulted from 'acts deliberately committed in order to make it unavoidable'.
2 Germany and Austria-Hungary deliberately worked to defeat 'all the many conciliatory proposals made by the Entente powers to avoid war'.[2]

The view of Germany as the story-book villain is enshrined in Article 231 of the Treaty of Versailles, which held Germany and its allies 'guilty' for starting the First World War.

During the inter-war years, the German government sought to reverse this verdict and released 15,889 official documents in 54 volumes during the 1920s to accomplish this end.[3] The weight of this evidence led many to alter their original views. David Lloyd George, the British prime minister, in his war memoirs, suggested that 'all the nations of Europe slithered over the edge of the boiling cauldron of war in 1914'.[4] In 1927, Erich Brandenburg, a German historian, argued that Germany did not plan for war in 1914. He blamed Russia for wanting control of the Balkans, and France for wanting revenge for the loss of Alsace-Lorraine.[5] In 1930, Sidney Fay, an American historian, published a balanced and deeply influential study, which argued that no European power wanted war in 1914 and that all, to greater or lesser degrees, must share the blame. Fay attached some liability to each power involved in the July Crisis. Germany did not plot the war and was a casualty of its alliance with Austria-Hungary. Austria-Hungary was most responsible, but felt that it was acting in self-defence against the expansion of Serb nationalism. Serbia may not have wanted war, but believed that it would be forced to fight. Russia was partly responsible, for encouraging Serbia and mobilising its troops. France can be blamed in a roundabout way for its determination to support Russia. Britain did make efforts for peace, but did hardly anything to restrain Russia or

France.[6] Thus, Fay concluded that the verdict of sole German guilt was defective.

Collective responsibility

The idea of collective responsibility for the outbreak of war soon became the orthodox interpretation. During the 1930s, the question of German guilt became a very sensitive issue in foreign relations, and was cordially dropped. In 1938, for example, G. P. Gooch, a leading British historian, reflected the prevailing orthodoxy by stating: 'The belief that any nation or statesman was the arch criminal in 1914 is no longer held by serious students of history.'[7] The debate had moved away from apportioning guilt towards an assessment of long-term causes. The inter-war period was the golden age of the study of international relations. Many specialists in this comparatively new subject held that the causes of war could be clearly isolated and future wars thereby prevented. Every type of long-term cause, including the alliance system and old-style diplomacy, imperial rivalry, the growth of militarism, nationalism, the arms race, and the development of inflexible war plans, was advanced.

After 1945, the focal point of the debate over war origins shifted to the Second World War. In 1951, however, a conference of French and German historians, organised by Gerhard Ritter, a leading German historian, met to reflect on the current state of the debate on the origins of the First World War and concluded: 'The documents do not permit attributing a premeditated desire for a European war on the part of any government or people in 1914. Distrust was at a peak, ruling circles were dominated by the idea that war was inevitable. Each one accused the other of aggressive intentions; each accepted the risk of war and saw its hope of security in the alliance system and the development of armaments.'[8]

During the 1960s, two American political scientists introduced a computer to the debate. A total of 5,000 key views, culled from all the verbatim documents of unquestioned authenticity of the key decision-makers in Germany, Russia, Austria-Hungary, Britain and France during the July Crisis of 1914, were fed into a computer, which came to these conclusions:

1 All the major powers felt that their rivals were antagonistic, and saw themselves as being friendly.
2 The major leaders became obsessed with short-term decisions during the July Crisis.
3 All the major powers felt that they were the injured party in the crisis.

The computer research confirmed that no one power was solely responsible for the outbreak of war.[9]

Germany and the origins of war: Fritz Fischer and his critics

In 1961, Fritz Fischer, a German historian, dropped a bombshell onto the debate by publishing a book 900 pages long, entitled, *Griff nach der Weltmacht*

('Grab for world power'). This was eventually published in English, with the more sober title: *Germany's aims in the First World War* (1967).[10] The book apportioned chief responsibility to Germany for preparing and launching the First World War. It was to provoke a fierce conflict between German historians. Fischer was an unusual revolutionary: born in 1908, he served in the German army during the Second World War, and was appointed professor of history at Hamburg University in 1948.

The Fischer thesis

Fischer's approach was very conventional, concentrating on the archives of the German leadership and focusing on the aims and policies of four key German figures: the Kaiser; Bethmann Hollweg, the chancellor; Gottlieb von Jagow, the foreign secretary; and Helmuth von Moltke, the chief of the army's general staff. Fischer believed that the truth about German guilt or innocence could only be determined by the official documents. He gained access to unpublished documents in East Germany. The major aim of the book was to show, in laborious detail, the vast, expansionist aims of Germany during the war. Only one chapter in the book deals with the origins of the war. Even so, the Fischer thesis is associated with the idea of German responsibility for the outbreak of war. On this issue, Fischer makes the following claims:

1 Germany was prepared to launch the First World War in order to become a great power.
2 Germany encouraged Austria-Hungary to start a war with Serbia, and continued to do so, even when it seemed clear that such a war could not be localised.
3 Once the war began, Germany developed a clear set of aims, already discussed before the war, to gain large territorial gains in central and eastern Europe, very similar to Hitler's later craving for *Lebensraum* ('living space') in eastern Europe.

The tremendous response to the book led Fischer to write a follow-up volume in 1969 entitled *Krieg der Illusionen* (published in English under the title *War of illusions*). This concentrated on German foreign policy from 1911 to 1914, and argued that the Kaiser's government cold-bloodedly planned the outbreak of the First World War from 1912 onwards.[11]

The two most unorthodox aspects of Fischer's thesis were the prominence given to domestic factors in shaping Germany's foreign policy (*Primat der Innenpolitik*), as opposed to the established German view that external factors shaped foreign policy (*Primat der Aussenpolitik*), and the new evidence that he assembled concerning the actions of Bethmann Hollweg, the German chancellor. The importance of domestic issues on the shaping of German foreign policy can be traced back to the influence of Eckart Kehr, a young radical German historian of the Weimar period, who argued that domestic factors were the chief moving force behind German foreign-policy adventures.[12] In a similar way, Fischer suggested that German foreign policy was viewed by the Kaiser and his government as a key means of diverting attention from domestic discontentment.

However, Fischer's most remarkable claims are reserved for Theobald Bethmann Hollweg. He was traditionally viewed as a cultured, responsible, well-meaning liberal statesman, who was surrounded by military hotheads during the July Crisis. In Fischer's view, Bethmann Hollweg was no puppet of the militarists, but the prime mover of German policy during the July Crisis of 1914, and a key figure in the development of Germany's expansionist aims once war began. Bethmann Hollweg was deeply gloomy about the Balkan situation, realised that Austria-Hungary required Germany's full support, and believed that Germany had to break free from its diplomatic 'encirclement'. To this end, the German chancellor attempted to improve Anglo-German relations, and hoped that the British government might remain neutral in any future war. The 'blank cheque' given to Austria-Hungary during the July Crisis, and Bethmann Hollweg's last-minute pleas for British neutrality, were therefore essential parts of a pre-existing German policy. Thus, Fischer believes that the First World War was no preventative war, born of fear and desperation; it was planned and launched by Germany with the aggressive aim of dominating Europe. If Fischer is correct, then Germany bears full responsibility for starting the First World War, and, as a result, Hitler cannot be seen as a ghost in the German machine – he was no crazed madman, but an ordinary German statesman whose aims and policies were not very different from those of Bethmann Hollweg, the German chancellor who went to war in 1914. Fischer sees a clear continuity in Germany foreign policy from the *Kaiserreich* (the empire) to Nazi Germany.[13]

Criticism of Fischer

Not surprisingly, the Fischer thesis triggered off one of the most intense debates on German history. The orthodox view, which had been so thought-fully constructed, of all the major European powers 'slithering over the brink into the boiling cauldron of war', was challenged. The majority of German historians managed to ignore the massive, three-volume work of Luigi Albertini, published in the 1950s, which had already suggested that Germany was the nation most responsible for the outbreak of the First World War,[14] and other works by non-German historians which argued much the same. But it was the Fischer thesis which caused the greatest reaction, because it was being advanced by a secure and highly respected doyen of traditional diplomatic history.

The views of Fischer were greeted with a harshness rarely seen, even among German historians. Fischer was accused of 'reading history backwards' for depicting imperial Germany as a breeding ground and source of influence for the later, expansionist aims of Hitler's Germany. Fischer's approach was also seen as contradictory. He focused on evidence from German 'high politics', but suggested that policy was affected by social and economic factors – which he ignored. The book was also accused of being 'Germanocentric', in so far as it

2 Bethmann Hollweg lacked the patience to settle matters by negotiation, believed that the Entente powers were paralysing Germany, and realised that Russia was growing stronger in the Balkans, and Austria-Hungary weaker.
3 When he gave Austria-Hungary the 'blank cheque', Bethmann Hollweg realised that the crisis might escalate into a European war.

Yet Zechlin is willing to accept that German policy took advantage of the Austro-Serb crisis to further its own aims. It seems that the Kaiser and his government hoped that the crisis might divide the Entente powers and give Germany a bloodless diplomatic victory. Only if this diplomatic bluff failed was war to be undertaken. This suggests that Germany went to war with the limited and defensive objective of breaking free of its diplomatic encirclement, not with the aim of acquiring vast territorial gains. Zechlin shows that Bethmann Hollweg desired a quick victory and a diplomatic settlement to replace the alliance system with a self-regulating balance of power in Europe.[22]

These views were given extra weight by Karl Erdmann, who found some new evidence of crucial importance which had been underplayed by Fischer. This was the diary of Kurt Reizler, private secretary to Bethmann Hollweg.[23] The Reizler diary reveals Bethmann Hollweg as someone who knew that any action by Austria-Hungary against Serbia might lead to war. The major issue for Germany was Austria-Hungary's status as a great power. There is no evidence in the diaries to indicate that Germany was systematically planning or preparing for the provocation of war. Even so, Erdmann is willing to accept that Germany took advantage of the Austro-Serb conflict to further its own aims. The major aim of Bethmann Hollweg was to disrupt the Entente through a bloodless diplomatic victory, if possible, or war if the Entente powers remained united. However, other historians have accused Erdmann of using the Reizler diary selectively, and have cast doubt on the authenticity of many of its entries, especially those from 6 to 23 July 1914.[24]

Despite this, Erdmann sticks by his interpretation, and rejects a number of Fritz Fischer's other claims. He shows the development of territorial aims to be a product of the war – not the fulfilment of a pre-war plan. He rejects the idea of the war being launched purely for economic, imperialist gains, and is unwilling to accept that the war was launched to escape from domestic problems. For Erdmann, the major German aims were limited to ensuring Austria-Hungary's survival as a major European power, and bringing about a re-ordering of the alliance system. Thus, the anti-Fischer school is willing to accept that Germany should take the major responsibility for the war, but rejects:

1 the view of German policy being determined by domestic difficulties;
2 the view that Germany was planning an aggressive war of expansion.

In place of this, it suggests that German leaders were gambling on a localised European war, with a swift German victory to break free from Germany's diplomatic 'encirclement'.

German domestic politics and the road to war

The most contested area of debate within the Fischer rumpus concerns the issue of whether the German government considered foreign policy in the light of domestic circumstances. The domestic politics of the *Kaiserreich* have been widely examined. V. R. Berghahn and Hans-Ulrich Wehler, keen supporters of Fischer, have shown how the aristocratic, Junker (Prussian landowning) elite supported an aggressive foreign policy as an escape from the political consequences of industrialisation, especially the desire for greater democracy in Germany. Wehler believes that Fischer's idea of continuity in German history from 1871 to 1914 is the best way in which to understand the origins of the First and Second World Wars.[25] Paul Kennedy has demonstrated how *Weltpolitik* was often used as a distraction from domestic problems and believes that fear of the Social Democrats was a contributory factor in the decision for war.[26] Arno Mayer has suggested that the German government hoped for great diplomatic and military victories with which to consolidate the monarchy, hold back reform, and prevent revolution.[27]

The entire debate over the role of domestic factors in German foreign policy has become very complex.[28] A chief historical concern is to explain whether Germany followed an exceptional path (*Sonderweg*), an idea supported by Ralf Dahrendorf, who suggested that Imperial Germany was an 'industrial feudal society' composed of a modern industrial economy which allowed for the survival of pre-industrial elites determined to hold back democratic development. The German middle class never gained a dominant position in German politics and remained subordinate to the Junker class, whose wealth was based on land. To justify the lack of democracy, the Kaiser and the Junkers devised complex strategies to weaken the influence of organised labour, and used foreign policy and imperialism to rally the middle class to support the ruling elite. This strategy, known as *Sammlungspolitik* (the politics of 'collection'), encouraged support for popular nationalist pressure groups, imperialist adventures and naval rivalry.[29] This view suggests that an unhealthy mixture of a modern society and a pre-industrial, ruling elite lay at the heart of why Germany embarked on *Weltpolitik* and decided on war in 1914.

However, Richard Evans and others have dismissed claims of a peculiar German way as being pure speculation.[30] The two best-known critics of this view are the British historians Geoffrey Eley and David Blackbourn, who strongly reject the idea of a unique German path towards democracy.[31] They also reject the idea that imperial Germany used war and foreign adventures to divert the masses from domestic problems. Blackbourn and Eley claim:

1 Germany did have a bourgeois revolution in the nineteenth century, and its society was 'modern', not 'semi-feudal'. In fact, Eley goes even further and suggests that a 'de facto parliamentary system' existed in Germany before 1914.
2 The German army was not monolithic, but was gradually incorporating members of the middle class into the officer ranks.

3 The idea of the German government using nationalism to divert attention from the growth of social democracy has been greatly exaggerated.
4 The German government did not regard war as the best way of resolving Germany's domestic difficulties.
5 A close examination of military, nationalistic and radical groups has shown that not all of them favoured an expansionist foreign policy.[32]

It does seem that the German leadership was not as concerned about using foreign policy as a diversion from domestic problems as is often routinely argued. The idea of 'a primacy of domestic politics' is being increasingly modified. David Kaiser has recently portrayed Bethmann Hollweg as someone who did not regard a major European war as a useful means of diverting attention from domestic difficulties. The socialist threat was not a major influence over the conduct of German foreign policy. Kaiser shows that Bethmann Hollweg believed that a protracted European war would be likely to destroy the monarchy – not strengthen it.[33] It is difficult to sustain the idea of the complete primacy of domestic politics even when it is applied just to German foreign policy. The theory is even less successful when applied to the other major European powers involved in the July Crisis.[34] It is very difficult to separate the external factors from internal factors. This may explain why many supporters of Fischer have called for a return to the analysis of the elite's reaction to the growing complexity of German society.

On the other hand, the complex picture of German society revealed by Fischer's critics can be used, in a roundabout way, to reinvigorate his thesis. The Reichstag (the German parliament), which favoured parties of the centre and left, did place restrictions on vastly increased military expenditure. From 1912 to 1914, deadlock existed in German politics between the Reichstag, which was growing in stature and which wanted to restrict military spending, and the Kaiser and his military leaders, who wanted to increase it. Thus, German domestic politics, with its bureaucratic infighting, was proving a handicap to militarists in the army and the navy. This may help to explain why the army so enthusiastically pushed for war in 1914, not to implement military plans, but to break free of domestic restrictions on increased armaments' expenditure. This puts the role of the army in 1914 back at the centre of interest. After all, it was only under conditions of war that the German army could gain access to the sort of spending resources required to take on the rest of Europe. Perhaps Berchtold, the Austrian foreign minister, had a point when he said 'Who rules in Berlin, Bethmann or Moltke?'[35] The 'militarism from above' was therefore more decisive regarding the actual decision for war in 1914, although the domestic political restraints on foreign policy may have provided the spur to action. In such a view, the 'militarism from below', most in evidence in the activities of right-wing pressure groups demanding a greater role for the army and navy, assumes much less importance. The whole debate has become excessively German-centred. As a result, the role of other factors in causing the war has been relegated to a subordinate position within the debate.

The nature of the international system: alliances and diplomacy

No explanation of why the European powers acted as they did in July 1914 can avoid some consideration of the nature and composition of the alliance system. Bernadotte Schmitt argued that the issue at stake during the July Crisis was a struggle to decide the balance of power in Europe for an indefinite time ahead between the Triple Alliance and the Triple Entente. Thus, in Schmitt's view, 'the alliances which had originally served the cause of peace, when put to the final test, almost mechanically operated to convert a local quarrel into a general war'.[36] This view once commanded widespread support. Indeed, few historians would disagree that the alliance system was important in encouraging the build-up of European tension. However, A. J. P. Taylor was probably right to claim that the pre-1914 alliances were so precarious and fragile that they cannot be seen as the major cause of the war.[37] This indicates that a fundamental problem which contributed to the outbreak of war was the *lack* of a fully effective balance of power in Europe – not its existence. Even a formal alliance in 1914 did not guarantee support for war. Italy, which had a binding alliance with Germany and Austria-Hungary, remained neutral. Britain, with no binding alliance – the Entente Cordiale of 1904 was a bond of friendship and settled colonial differences – decided to go to war.

The crucial alliances were the German alliance with Austria-Hungary and the Franco-Russian alliance. Germany was determined to support its alliance partner throughout the crisis, but was clearly following its own aims. The French did clearly offer support for its alliance partner, but did not play a crucial role in the decision for war. Thus, alliances were important, but as James Joll has argued, no European power really accepted that the alliance system consisted of two firm and balanced power blocs, and no major European power subscribed to the idea that the alliance system was a complete deterrent against war.[38] Each power made wrong calculations about the likely behaviour of its alliance opponents. The pre-1914 alliance system was therefore a very fragile system but it did not make war inevitable. It seems that the alliance system raised expectations about likely allies in a future war, and influenced the military plans of each power. However, each nation seemed to base its decision for war on an assessment of national interests, which were linked to alliances, but were not, in all cases, determined by them.

War by timetable? Militarism, armaments and war plans

It has often been claimed that a mood of militarism pervaded Europe before 1914. Hence, militarism, armaments and the war plans of the major powers have all been put forward as key factors in the outbreak of war. Europe has been viewed as 'an armed camp' from 1870 to 1914. Michael Howard argues that each announcement of increased armaments' expenditure by a European power before 1914 was viewed as a threat by its perceived rival, and thus created an atmosphere of mutual fear and suspicion which played a major part in creating the mood for war in 1914.[39] The view that the First World War was brought about by the escalation of an arms race is superficially attractive. Yet the idea that a build-up of arms naturally leads to war remains dubious. In fact, the proportion of the gross domestic product (GDP) spent by the major European powers on arms expenditure was quite small. In 1914, Germany spent 3.5 per cent of GDP on defence; this was less than Britain (4.9 per cent), France (3.9 per cent) and Russia (4.6 per cent). The belief that high expenditure on arms leads to a desire for war remains unproved. For example, Austria-Hungary (1.9 per cent) spent less than all the major powers on arms in 1914, but was determined to go to war. In a recent summary of the debate, Niall Ferguson has claimed that the role of the arms race in encouraging the First World War has been greatly exaggerated.[40] The country with the largest growth in military expenditure before 1914 was Britain – the power which least wanted war. Most European nations spent far more on education and social services than on armaments.

Many historians believe that the considerations of the leading powers regarding the strategic balance of power was a much greater influence on policy during the July Crisis. According to L. F. C. Turner, the crisis cannot be understood without knowledge of the balance of military power, military planning and military strategy.[41] The balance of power in the Balkans was turning sharply against Austria-Hungary. This was a vital factor to the Austro-Hungarian chiefs of staff, who argued for a 'preventative war' to weaken Serbia.[42] Similarly, the German chiefs of staff had grown pessimistic about Germany's strategic position, were obsessed with the growing strength of the French and Russian armies in Europe, and believed that the balance of power was moving sharply away from Germany. This led them to suggest that it was better for Germany to fight a war sooner rather than later.

Strategic fears were closely linked to military aims and plans. A. J. P. Taylor argued that the outbreak of the First World War was caused 'almost entirely by rival plans for mobilisation by the European powers'. This view has many supporters.[43] All the European powers had developed detailed war plans in the expectation of war. The military planners believed in a swift mobilisation of forces and lightning offensives. Yet the relationship between military plans and the actual decision for war is notoriously complicated. In Britain, Sir Edward Grey took hardly any notice of army and naval chiefs when considering British participation in the First World War. The French government did not really support the idea of an offensive strategy, and was not greatly influenced by the military planners anyway. In Russia, the chiefs of staff told the Tsar that the army was ready for war, and the Russian emperor and his ministers made the decision to mobilise forces. Military planning was more influential in Austria-Hungary and Germany. The Austro-Hungarian chiefs of staff persuaded the Habsburg government that a lightning assault against Serbia was required. The German generals strongly advised the Kaiser and his government to implement the Schlieffen Plan. This involved a war on two fronts and a speedy offensive.

However, recent studies show that the plans of the German army were in harmony with the foreign-policy objectives of the government; the military planners were telling the Kaiser and his government what they wanted to hear. It was the major leaders – not the soldiers – who took the final decisions. Even so, it was in Germany and Austria-Hungary that the military planners seem to have had the most decisive influence over foreign policy.

Nationalism

The role of national self-determination in the origins of the war has been another important area of debate. Martel has argued that the First World War grew out of a clash between 'Slav nationalism' and the multi-ethnic Austro-Hungarian Empire. The assassination of Archduke Franz Ferdinand was the final straw in this struggle for mastery in the Balkans. It offered the Austro-Hungarian government an ideal opportunity to rouse public opinion in support of a war which aimed to weaken the drive for self-determination in the Balkans.[44] This type of interpretation, which sets the July Crisis in the context of the long-running 'Eastern Question', views the First World War as one which was fought for the future of central and eastern Europe.[45]

Very few historians would object to the view that the struggle to supplant the Ottoman Empire in the Balkans was a very important factor in the outbreak of war. The key players in this struggle were southern European nationalist groups, Russia (which hoped to profit from the Ottoman decline) and Austria-Hungary (which feared Slav nationalism and Russian ambitions). In July 1914, the military leaders of Austria-Hungary were so determined to deal with Serbia that they lost their heads, persisted with a disastrous ultimatum, and ignored all pleas for mediation. The level of fear and emotion that Slav nationalism caused in Austria-Hungary should not be underestimated.[46]

In Joachim Remak's view, the Habsburg–Serb quarrel was not a minor issue, but the major issue which brought about war. The rest of Europe was dragged into what Remak terms 'the third Balkan War'.[47] He argues that Austria-Hungary and Serbia both knew that they were on a collision course in 1914, and that they did not care if their battle for supremacy in the Balkans activated all the major European alliances. According to this view, primary responsibility for beginning the war is shared between Austria-Hungary, which wanted to restore its prestige, and Serbia, which stood in a good position to benefit from European rivalry in the region. The growth of Serbia clearly threatened the future of the Habsburg Empire. The delivery of the Austrian ultimatum and the decision to attack Serbia were also crucial points on the road to war. The view that Austria-Hungary was solely responsible has also been strongly argued by many historians.

However, the pioneering work of John Leslie, a British historian whose knowledge of the documents on Austria-Hungary was matchless, has cast great doubt on the importance of the Austro-Serb quarrel. Leslie makes three crucial points:

1 Austria-Hungary used the assassination of Archduke Franz Ferdinand as an excuse to settle accounts with Serbia, and asked Germany to prevent Russian intervention.
2 Germany saw the war with Serbia as secondary to the struggle with Russia.
3 In the July Crisis, the Kaiser virtually commanded Austria-Hungary to set aside its anger against Serbia and to deploy the major portion of its troops against Russia.

Thus, Leslie believes that Austria-Hungary can be held responsible for planning a local Austro-Serb conflict, which was linked to its fears about Balkan nationalism, but Germany, which was not interested in this quarrel, quite deliberately used it as an opportunity to launch the European war which Austria-Hungary had never desired.[48] A recent investigation into the policy of Serbia shows no plan for a third Balkan war. On the contrary, it seems that Serbia was exhausted by the previous Balkan struggles, and desired a period of stability and a peaceful settlement of the July Crisis.[49] John Lowe perhaps puts the significance of the Austro-Serb quarrel into its proper context by stating: 'The crisis in the Balkans was the occasion, rather than the cause of the First World War.'[50]

An imperialist war? Marxist and economic explanations

The Marxist-Leninist view

The role of imperialism and economic factors in the origins of the First World War has not greatly attracted historians in recent years. It was once argued by Marxist writers and historians that imperial rivalry and the influence of monopoly capital were major underlying reasons for the war. The first serious attempt to explain the role of imperialism was put forward by V. I. Lenin, the leader of the Russian Bolshevik Party, in *Imperialism: the highest stage of capitalism*, written in exile during 1916.[51] This interpretation saw the war as being the direct consequence of imperial rivalry, which led capitalist businessmen to seek new markets and encouraged governments to support economic interests. Lenin believed that German monopoly capital was behind German foreign policy. The primary aim was to gain territory denied to Germany during the era of the 'new imperialism'. Lenin saw war as inherent in the nature of capitalism. In this way, the First World War can be seen as the culmination of a search for territory and markets, led by capitalists whose aims were supported by governments. In this view, millions of people were being sacrificed to ensure the future domination of one group of monopoly capitalists over another. However, it should be said that the scramble for territory in Africa and Asia never led to war between the major European powers, and very rarely threatened to do so.

Marxist-Leninist theory also insisted that the foreign policies of the major European powers were a function of capitalist businessmen. Many Marxist historians saw monopoly capital as the hidden hand behind the First World

War. A typical example of this sort of interpretation was advanced by Konne Zilliacus shortly after the Second World War, who argued that no European nation went to war in 1914 because of treaty obligations, moral issues or the rights of small nations, but to defend imperialist interests, which consisted of 'the private interests of finance and monopoly capital'.[52] Yet It seems clear that major western European industries, especially steel, iron and coal, were becoming interdependent before 1914, and that among capitalist businessmen involved in such industries there was a desire for peace.[53]

The Marxist-Leninist explanation has never achieved general acceptance among the majority of traditional historians. It remains difficult to find convincing evidence for the Influence of capitalist businessmen on the foreign policy of the major European powers before 1914. Indeed, the aims of government and business are often deeply divided. In August 1914, for example, a delegation of leading financiers from the City of London begged Sir Edward Grey not to go to war, but he ignored them. Similarly, not all German monopoly capitalists supported war in 1914. For example, Albert Ballin and Max Warburg, two seemingly 'ideal type' German capitalists, opposed the war. On the other hand, many arms manufacturers and steel companies did make enormous profits from war, but they also made profits in peacetime. Bankers and arms manufacturers did have influence over foreign policy, but did not always advocate war. A great many Marxist explanations regarding the role of economics on war are all too often based on speculation, guesswork and a very partial reading (or often total neglect) of original sources.

However, the rejection of purely Marxist-Leninist interpretations of the origin of the war should not lead to a rejection of the importance of economic considerations *per se*. A strong industrial economy did prove vital to a successful foreign policy in the twentieth century. The role of economics was obviously a deeply important 'unspoken assumption' of the policy-makers. But the link between politics and economic factors has generally been ignored by diplomatic historians, who have relied on the 'official records' of government as the basic source used for analysis.[54] Official sources tend to discuss a particular policy that is to be adopted, not the ways in which business groups or economic factors have influenced the chosen course of action. According to Joll, 'official records' are often based on conventions which exclude the importance of business influence.[55] Even so, it must be conceded that there is no evidence that there was any business interest in planning a war in 1914. It is therefore difficult to claim that the pressure for war in 1914 came from capitalist interests.

Modern economic considerations

However, Paul Kennedy, a leading diplomatic historian, has recently suggested that 'economic' interests are a key 'reality behind diplomacy'.[56] In this view, politicians have autonomous freedom to pursue foreign policy – even to make the vital decision for war – without reference to economic interest groups within society. However, the economic and industrial resources of each nation ultimately determine the success or failure of those decisions. In other words, politicians have the primacy of political decisions for war, but no control over the economic consequences of such decisions. This implies that economics plays a vital role in deciding the fate of nations within the international system. In Kennedy's view, economic strength is woven into the fabric of great power struggles.[57]

Another important new approach is to examine the origins of the First World War within the context of the relationship between power politics and economic power. The work of Carl Stirkwerda on the relationship between European governments and industry is a very important contribution to this area of study. Stirkwerda argues that the crisis of 1914 must be understood within a framework which investigates whether all European leaders actually believed that political and military power were essential to economic success. Stirkwerda shows a very high level of economic co-operation and integration in Europe prior to 1914. For example, 221 new international organisations were founded between 1900 and 1914. It seems that international economic relations before 1914 were not as ridden with conflict as was previously supposed. Most industrialists desired mutually beneficial economic relations, and many wanted greater economic integration within European trade and financial sectors. Even in Germany, Hugo Stinnes, a major industrialist, said in 1911: 'three to four years of peace, and I can guarantee the silent German domination of Europe'. In other words, many German industrialists saw no need for war. However, it was not industrialists who had the most significant influence over foreign policy, but political leaders.

The German leadership never fully defined what sorts of long-term economic gains would be achieved by war. In Britain and France, there was a clear realisation that a war would lead to serious economic difficulties. The tsarist regime also worried about the economic consequences of the war. This realisation should have led to a greater desire to appease any likely warmonger in 1914, but the decision-makers never saw peace and economic co-operation as something to be achieved 'without honour' or at any price. 'The disaster of 1914', writes Paul Schroeder, 'did not derive from a failure of politicians, military men, various interest groups and the broad public to appreciate the long-range advantages of peaceful international co-operation over un-restrained competition and conflict. It lay rather in the structure of international politics – the fact that individual states would not, and could not, either separately or together leap from a power-based competitive system to a rule-based one'.[58] This serves to remind us that the structure of international power politics, not economic factors, was the central determinant of the outbreak of the First World War.[59]

The 'mood of the age' was dominated by power-political considerations: alliances, military plans and military strength, not the modern-day desire for a mutually beneficial economic environment in which all nations will reap benefits. Indeed, the influence of economic co-operation was hardly influential at all in eastern Europe – the very area in which the crisis of 1914 erupted. It seems that leaders in 1914 did not really understand the advantages of economic co-operation and integration. Most European governments, with the exception of Britain, had adopted protectionism, believing that this offered a better insurance against economic depression. Perhaps we should be asking why the leaders in 1914 thought the way they did, and surveying the differences between the assumptions of government and the needs of business, as many historians are attempting in other historical fields of study.[60]

The orthodox view

- The outbreak of the war was the collective responsibility of all the belligerents.

Fischer's view

- The continuity of German history from 1871 to 1914 led to war.
- The German desire for territorial expansion led to war.
- The German desire to break free of its diplomatic encirclement led to war.
- The war was a way of diverting the German populace from domestic problems.

Ritter's view

- Germany had no desire for world dominion; its main aim was to support its ally, Austria-Hungary.
- German military planners pushed Germany into war.

Other views

- Germany intended only a defensive, or 'preventative', war.
- Germany went to war to achieve the aims of *Weltpolitik*.
- Germany wanted war to reorder the alliance system.
- Germany wanted war in the interests of *Sammlungspolitik*.
- Imperial rivalry encouraged German monopoly capitalists to push for new territory and markets by means of war.
- Germany wanted to swing the European balance of power in its favour by war.
- Austria-Hungary's desire to crush nationalist movements in Serbia led to war.
- The rival plans for mobilisation of the European powers led to war.

Figure 1. The historians' debates over the origins of the First World War.

Notes and references

1 The changing nature of the debate is expertly summarised in J. Langdon, *July 1914, the long debate, 1918–90*, Oxford, 1991. See also H. Strachen, 'The First World War: causes and course', *Historical Journal*, vol. 29 (1986).

2 D. E. Lee, *The outbreak of the First World War: who was responsible?*, London, 1963, p. 4.

3 See E. T. S. Dugdale (ed.), *German diplomatic documents: 1871–1914*, 4 vols., London, 1928.

4 D. Lloyd George, *War memoirs*, vol. 2, London, 1933, p. 52.

5 E. Brandenburg, *From Bismarck to the world war*, Oxford, 1927.

6 S. B. Fay, *Origins of the world war*, 2 vols., London, 1930.

7 G. P. Gooch, *Before the war: the coming of war*, vol. 2, London, 1938.

8 J. A. Corbett, 'France and Germany agree – on the past', *Historical Bulletin*, vol. 27 (1955), pp. 158–62.

9 R. O. Holsti and R. C. North, 'The history of human conflict', in E. B. McNeil (ed.), *The nature of human conflict*, New Jersey, 1965.

10 F. Fischer, *Germany's aims in the First World War*, London, 1967. This is the English translation of *Griff nach der Weltmacht* (1961). For a summary of the Fischer controversy, see J. A. Moses, *The politics of illusion: the Fischer controversy in German historiography*, London, 1975. See also, R. Fletcher, 'Introduction' to F. Fischer, *from Kaiserreich to Third Reich: elements of continuity in German history, 1871–1945*, London, 1986. For a balanced assessment of recent trends on the question of German policy, see N. Ferguson, 'Germany and the origins of the First World War: new perspectives', *Historical Journal*, vol. 35 (1992).

11 F. Fischer, *War of illusions*, London, 1975. See also H. Hantsch, 'The debate on the July Crisis continues: Professor Fischer's second volume and its aftermath', *European Studies Review*, vol. 1 (1971).

12 See A. L. Skop. 'The primacy of domestic politics: Eckart Kehr and the intellectual development of Charles A. Beard', *History and Theory*, vol.13 (1974).

13 The debate over continuity is thoroughly examined in R. J. W. Evans, 'From Hitler to Bismarck: Third Reich and Kaiserreich in recent historiography', *Historical Journal*, vol. 26 (1984).

14 L. Albertini, *The origins of the war of 1914*, 3 vols., Oxford, 1952–57.

15 For a discussion of Ritter's criticism of the Fischer thesis, see K. H. Janssen, 'Gerhard Ritter: a patriotic historian's justification', in H. W. Koch (ed.), *The origins of the First World War*, London, 1984.

16 This summary of Ritter's views is taken from G. Ritter, *The sword and the sceptre: the problem of militarism in Germany*, 4 vols., London, 1971–74.

17 Stephen van Evera has recently written: 'I am satisfied the "Fischer School" have proven their argument that German pre-war intentions were aggressive'. See S. van Evera, 'Why co-operation failed in 1914', *World Politics*, vol. 38 (1985). Other historians are more pessimistic as to whether Fischer has won the day, even on the question of German responsibility in 1914.

18 I have used the views of Geiss as a leading example of the supporters of Fritz Fischer. See I. Geiss, *German foreign policy, 1871–1914*, London, 1976. There are many other leading 'Fischerites', including Hans-Ulrich Wehler, V. R. Berghahn, Arno Mayer and J. Kocka. However, the distinctions between the Fischer and anti-Fischer schools have recently become blurred as the debate evolves. For a discussion of the major views of the so-called 'Fischer school', see R. Fletcher, 'Recent developments in West German historiography: the Bielefeld school and its critics', *German Studies Review*, vol. 7 (1984). For a balanced judgement of the Fischer controversy, see R. G. Moeller, 'The Kaiserreich recast? Continuity and change in modern German historiography', *Journal of Social History*, vol. 17 (1984).

19 See I. Geiss, 'Origins of the First World War', in Koch (ed.), *Origins*.

20 See J. C. G. Röhl and N. Sombart (eds.), *Kaiser Wilhelm II: new interpretations*, Cambridge, 1982.

21 There are a long list of critics of Fischer, but Erdmann and Zechlin's criticisms of Fischer's view of German conduct during the July Crisis are representative. Another bitter German critic of Fischer is Andreas Hillgruber.

22 See E. Zechlin, 'Cabinet versus economic warfare in Germany: policy and strategy during the early months of the First World War' and E. Zechlin, 'July 1914: reply to a polemic', which can be found in Koch (ed.), *Origins*. The idea of Bethmann Hollweg taking a 'calculated risk' in 1914 is advanced in Konrad H. Jarausch, 'The illusion of limited war: Chancellor Bethmann Hollweg's calculated risk, July 1914', *Central European History*, vol. 2 (1969).

23 The Reizler diary is in a German edition. See K. Erdmann (ed.), *Kurt Reizler*, Göttingen, 1972. However, Erdmann outlines his major findings in K. Erdmann, 'War guilt 1914 reconsidered: a balance of new research', in Koch (ed.), *Origins*.

24 Two German historians, Bernard Sosemen and Fritz Fellner, have cast doubt on the authenticity of the Reizler diaries. The validity of the entries from 6 July to 23 August 1914 have been called into question. It does seem a bit old-fashioned to base a complete analysis of German policy in July 1914 on the entries of one diary.

25 Hans-Ulrich Wehler is the major defender of Fischer's view of the importance of domestic factors on German foreign policy. See H-U. Wehler, *The German Empire, 1871–1918*, Leamington Spa, 1985. See also W. Mommsen, 'The debate on German war aims', *Journal of Contemporary History*, vol. 1 (1966).

26 P. M. Kennedy, *The rise of the Anglo-German antagonism, 1860–1914*, London, 1980.

27 A. Mayer, 'Domestic origins of the First World War', in L. Krieger and F. Stern (eds.), *The responsibilities of power*, New York, 1967.

28 See W. Mommsen, 'Domestic factors in German foreign policy before 1914', *Central European History*, vol. 6 (1973).

29 See R. Dahrendorf, *Society and democracy in Germany*, London, 1966.

30 See R. J. W. Evans and H. P. von Strandmann (eds.), *The causes of the First World War*, Oxford, 1988.

31 See J. Kocka, 'German history before Hitler: the debate about the German *Sonderweg*', *Journal of Contemporary History*, vol. 23 (1988). A major attack on the idea of a unique German path can be found in D. Calleo, *The German problem reconsidered*, Cambridge, 1978.

32 D. Blackbourn and G. Eley, *The peculiarities of German history: bourgeois society and politics in nineteenth-century Germany*, Oxford, 1984. See also G. Eley, *Reshaping the German right: radical nationalism and political change after Bismarck*, New Haven, 1980; G. Eley, 'Recent work in modern German history', *Historical Journal*', vol. 23 (1980); and D. Blackbourn, *Class, religion and local politics in Wilhelmine Germany: the Centre Party in Wittenberg before 1914*, New Haven, 1980.

33 D. Kaiser, 'Germany and the origins of the First World War', *Journal of Modern History*, vol. 55 (1983).

34 A series of detailed studies of the other major European states in the July Crisis have all rejected the Fischer thesis. For example, Z. Steiner, *Britain and the origins of the First World War*, London, 1977, shows that British foreign policy was controlled by Sir Edward Grey and the Foreign Office, with domestic issues having very little influence. J. F. C. Kieger, in *France and the origins of the First World War*, London, 1983, argues that French policy was guided by external and strategic considerations, most notably the alliance with Russia and the Anglo-French Entente, and not domestic factors. The role of Russia has been

extensively examined in D. C. Lieven, *Russia and the origins of the First World War*, London, 1983, which concludes that Russia went to war to maintain the balance of power in Europe – not for domestic reasons.

35 Quoted in J. Lowe, *The great powers, imperialism and the German problem*, London, 1994, p. 229.

36 B. Schmitt, 'The origins of the First World War', in Lee (ed.), *Outbreak*, p. 79.

37 A. J. P. Taylor, 'The outbreak of war', in Lee (ed.), *Outbreak*, p. 56.

38 J. Joll, *The origins of the First World War*, London, 1984, pp. 34–57.

39 M. Howard (ed.), *The theory and practice of war: essays presented to B. H. Liddell Hart*, London, 1965.

40 Ferguson, 'Germany'.

41 L. F. C. Turner, *Origins of the First World War*, London, 1970, p. 113.

42 N. Stone, 'Army and society in the Habsburg monarchy, 1900–14', *Past and Present*, no. 33 (1966). See also N. Stone, 'Moltke–Conrad: relations between the Austro-Hungarian and German general staffs, 1909–14', *Journal of Contemporary History*, vol. 1 (1966).

43 A. J. P. Taylor, *War by timetable: how the First World War began*, London, 1969. This argument is also strongly advanced in J. Snyder, *The ideology of the offensive, military decision-making and the disasters of 1914*, Cornell, 1984.

44 G. Martel, *The origins of the First World War*, London, 1987, pp. 72–77.

45 M. S. Anderson, *The Eastern Question*, London, 1966. See also D. Dakin, 'The diplomacy of the great powers and the Balkan states, 1908–14', *Balkan Studies*, vol. 3 (1962).

46 It has been said that if Germany gave the 'blank cheque' Austria-Hungary tried to cash it. Certainly, Norman Stone, Sidney Fay and many others have assigned the primary responsibility for the escalation of the crisis to Austria-Hungary. See, for example, S. R. Williamson, *Austria-Hungary and the origins of the First World War*, London, 1991.

47 See J. Remak, '1914– the Third Balkan war: origins reconsidered', in Koch, *Origins*.

48 See F. Fellner, 'Austria-Hungary', in K .M. Wilson (ed.), *1914: decisions for war*, London, 1995.

49 See Wilson (ed.), *1914*.

50 Lowe, *Great powers*, p. 235.

51 V. I. Lenin, *Imperialism: the highest stage of capitalism*, 1916.

52 E. Zilliacus, 'Economic and social causes of the war', in Lee (ed.), *Outbreak*.

53 C. Stirkwerda, 'The troubled origins of European economic integration: international iron and steel and labor migration in the era of World War I', *American Historical Review*, vol. 98 (1993).

54 Stalin reportedly called traditional historians who based their arguments on official records 'archive rats'.

55 The whole question is examined fully in Joll, *Origins*, pp. 123–70.

56 P. M. Kennedy, *The realities behind diplomacy*, London, 1981.

57 This argument is advanced in P. M. Kennedy, *The rise and fall of the great powers*, London, 1988.

58 P. W. Schroeder, 'Economic integration and the European international system in the era of World War I', *American Historical Review*, vol. 98 (1993).

59 K. Waltz, *Theory of international politics*, Reading, 1979.

60 See N. J. White, 'Government and business divided: Malaya, 1945–57', *Journal of Imperial and Commonwealth History*, vol. 22 (1994).

3 The origins of the Second World War: 1 War and the fragile peace, 1914–33

A full understanding of the origins of the Second World War requires a detailed examination of the evolution of international relations before 1933. During this period, the international system underwent enormous changes. One of the most important was the development of a popular mood against the horrors of war. In 1931, for example, a leading statesman told the League of Nations Assembly: 'There has scarcely been a period in the world's history when war seemed less likely than it does at present.'[1] Anti-war films, poetry, novels and plays enjoyed widespread popularity. In 1932, the major world powers converged on Geneva for the World Disarmament Conference. However, a close examination of the period from 1914 to 1933 reveals that the popular mood against war, which developed after 1918, did not alter the selfish desires of nation states.

The ordeal of war, 1914–18

Every country was affected in some way by the First World War, and its legacy hung like a shadow over international relations during the inter-war period. Over 60 million Europeans fought in the war, 7 million died, and 21 million were disabled or seriously wounded. Over 4 million women lost husbands, and 8 million children lost fathers. One estimate puts the total loss of property at £30,000 million; in France, 250,000 buildings were destroyed, 500,000 damaged, and 6,000 square miles of territory devastated. The total estimated cost of the war has been put at £260,000 million.

Early predictions of a swift victory for the Triple Entente allies (Britain, France and Russia) or for the Central powers (Germany and Austria-Hungary) were overoptimistic. The German attack on France was halted at the Battle of Marne in September 1914. Soldiers then set about digging a line of trenches, separated by a barbed-wire-fenced 'no man's land', that stretched from the Swiss border to the English Channel. For most of the time, 'all was quiet on the Western Front', except for several attempts to break the deadlock, most notably at the battles of Verdun (1916), the Somme (1916) and Passchendaele (1917), which all produced enormous casualties but no decisive victory.

The high death toll placed strain on all the major powers. Events on the battlefield were directly felt by families on the 'home front'. The stalemate placed a high premium on the economy, and on the organisational abilities of

von Hindenburg, the leading German generals, decided that the best course for Germany to follow was for a new democratic government, not the army, to negotiate the peace terms. This decision helped to feed a powerful myth that Germany's army was not defeated in battle, but was 'stabbed in the back' by socialists and democrats at home. The Kaiser abdicated and fled into exile in The Netherlands. A new German democratic government was formed. At exactly 11 a.m. on 11 November 1918, the armistice was signed, and the First World War ended with a comprehensive German defeat.[2]

The Paris Peace Settlement and its consequences

On 12 January 1919, at the Palace of Versailles, the first session of the Paris Peace Conference began. Leaders from 32 nations were present to discuss the terms to be imposed on the defeated Central powers (Germany, Austria-Hungary, Bulgaria and Turkey). All the major decisions of the conference were made by the 'Council of Four', represented by the respective Allied leaders – David Lloyd George (Britain), Woodrow Wilson (the USA), Georges Clemenceau (France) and Vittorio Orlando (Italy). Representatives of 28 other Allied nations were also present, but the Soviet Union, now in diplomatic isolation, was not invited. The two major aims of the peacemakers were to bring political order to European politics, and to prevent such a catastrophe ever happening again.[3]

Europe in ruins

A number of very difficult problems confronted the peacemakers. The old European balance of power was in ruins. Four great, monarchical empires – imperial Germany (ruled by the Hohenzollern dynasty), Austria-Hungary (Habsburg), Turkey (Ottoman) and Russia (Romanov) – lay shattered, and a bewildering range of diverse nationalities in central and eastern Europe demanded national self-determination. The Russian Revolution caused deep anxieties amongst the peacemakers concerning the possibility of a communist revolution spreading throughout Europe.

Deep economic problems, most notably a collapse of world trade, unstable currencies, unemployment, agricultural depression and mounting debts, also aroused concern. Britain, France and Italy owed enormous sums in war debts alone. The material damage – devastated towns, blown-up railways and roads, destroyed houses, farms and livestock, and the merchant ships at the bottom of the sea – was equally devastating. Only two nations – the USA and Japan – profited from the war economically: the USA had become the world's major financial creditor, and Japanese industry was rapidly growing. To make matters worse, Europe's export market had virtually collapsed, and inflation was rising everywhere. In Germany, prices were five times higher than in 1914, in Austria-Hungary they were 14,000 times higher, and in Russia 4,000 million times higher. Industrial production in Europe in 1919 was 30 per cent below the pre-war level.

Psychological wounds also required healing. Coping with war on this scale proved to be extremely difficult. A total of 13 million people were killed, severely wounded or permanently disabled. This led to two types of reaction: popular demands by many in the victorious countries to 'make Germany pay'; and in Germany movements of former soldiers calling for vengeance. The popular press in Britain screeched the headlines 'Squeeze the German lemon till the pips squeak' and 'Hang the Kaiser'. This atmosphere made a lenient settlement much less likely.

The aims of the Allies

The four major victorious powers came to Paris with no agreed agenda, apart from Wilson's famous 'Fourteen Points'. The US president believed that the outbreak of the war was due to three central causes: the secretive and selfish nature of European diplomacy; the tendency of larger powers to deny ethnic minorities self-determination; and autocratic regimes which ignored the wishes of the people. Remove these three impediments to peace, he believed, and a new order of international relations could be created, based on principles of open diplomacy, national self-determination and democracy. Such high moral principles seemed idealistic when compared to old-fashioned European diplomacy. However, Wilson proved less than completely faithful to his principles. There was very little democracy about the decision-making process at Versailles. The 'Council of Four' took all the decisions in closed sessions.

Clemenceau is often regarded as being the chief architect of a harsh settlement with regard to Germany. The French obsession with security at the conference was due to three factors: the long French frontier with Germany; the loss of Russia as a balance to German power in eastern Europe; and the alarming differences between France and Germany's population and industrial potential. In fact, Clemenceau believed that the gravest mistake that the peacemakers could make would be to make 'excessive demands' on Germany. The French desired two guarantees of future security against a possible German revival: first, the demilitarisation of the region sandwiched between the German–French border known as the Rhineland; second, severe restrictions on German military power. In addition, the French sought financial assistance to rebuild its shattered territory. However, the French only pushed for a high reparations settlement when their own demand for a cancellation of war debts was rejected by the US and Britain. 'Every effort must be made to be just towards the Germans', said Clemenceau, 'but when it comes to persuading them that we are just towards them, that is another matter.'[4]

Lloyd George was primarily concerned about achieving a peace settlement which both reconstructed Europe and ensured that any future British involvement in European affairs would be limited. The defeat of Germany had achieved all of Britain's war aims: the German naval threat was destroyed, the German military threat was apparently defeated, and the German colonial threat was over. This allowed Lloyd George to revert to the old idea of Britain taking a middle position within the European balance of power. As France was now the dominant military power, this meant taking a conciliatory attitude towards Germany. As a result, the British delegation wanted military restrictions placed on Germany, some limited financial compensation, but not a totally punitive settlement. Many economic experts in the British delegation, including John Maynard Keynes, the brilliant young economist, saw German economic revival as vital for the recovery of Britain's European export trade, and argued against a harsh reparations settlement.

Orlando, the Italian premier, was largely ignored by the three major powers, and proved ineffective. The Italian delegation wanted to gain territory as compensation for entering the war on the Allied side in 1915 and suffering heavy losses. However, Orlando was unable to gain the port of Fiume, Italy's prime territorial objective. The row over Fiume resulted in the Italian delegation walking out of the conference, and led to the fall of Orlando's government. The denial of Fiume became a passionate nationalist issue in Italian politics. In 1919, Gabriele d'Annunzio, an Italian poet, formed a legion of nationalist agitators who seized the port and declared it a 'free city'. With problems at home and abroad, the Italian democratic government became deeply unpopular. It was eventually overthrown by Benito Mussolini, leader of the deeply nationalist Fascist Party, in 1922. During the inter-war period, fascism became a popular and despotic alternative to weak democratic governments in a state of deep economic and political crisis.

The Treaty of Versailles

Five separate treaties made up the final Paris Peace Settlement, but the Treaty of Versailles, signed by Germany in the historic Hall of Mirrors at the Palace of Versailles on 28 June 1919, was the most significant and controversial. German military power, the chief cause of the war, was the dominant issue at the peace conference. Germany had come very close to victory, and most of its industry had remained untouched. Unless the peacemakers took adequate precautions, there was every prospect of a German military revival. To prevent this, a number of arms limitations were implemented. The German army was limited to 100,000 men, conscription was abolished, and tanks and aircraft were prohibited. The navy was slimmed down to a coastal force of 36 vessels, and the building of battleships and submarines was outlawed. By these measures, the German army was reduced to the level of that of Greece, and the German navy was left on a par with Argentina's fleet.

Germany lost 13 per cent of its territory, including Alsace-Lorraine, Eupen, Malmédy, North Schleswig, West Prussia and Posen (Poznań). The loss of territory in eastern Europe was particularly bitterly criticised by the German government. Danzig (Gdańsk) became a 'free city', linked by a customs union to the new Polish state, which also gained Upper Silesia, a major industrial area. The Poles were additionally given a 'corridor' of land to the sea, which cut off East Prussia from the rest of Germany. In western Europe, the French got what they wanted: they gained Alsace-Lorraine; the Rhineland was made

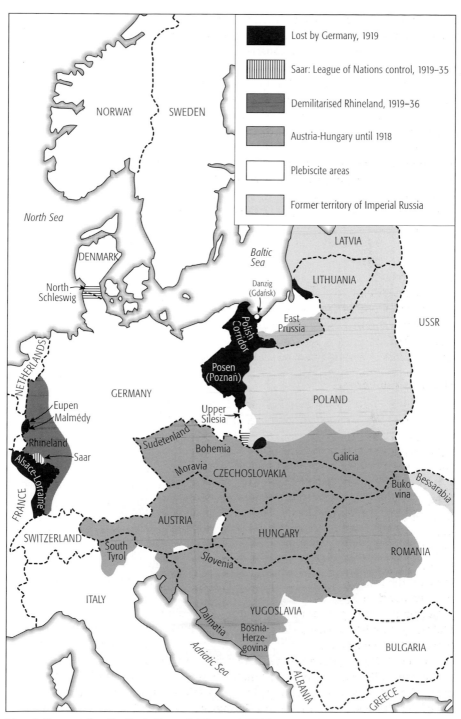

Map 4. Europe after the Paris Peace Settlement, 1919.

Legend:

- Lost by Germany, 1919
- Saar: League of Nations control, 1919–35
- Demilitarised Rhineland, 1919–36
- Austria-Hungary until 1918
- Plebiscite areas
- Former territory of Imperial Russia

NORWAY

SWEDEN

North Sea

DENMARK

Baltic Sea

LATVIA

LITHUANIA

USSR

North Schleswig

Danzig (Gdańsk)

East Prussia

NETHERLANDS

GERMANY

Polish Corridor

Posen (Poznań)

POLAND

Eupen Malmédy

Upper Silesia

Rhineland

Sudetenland

Bohemia

Galicia

Bessarabia

Saar

Moravia

CZECHOSLOVAKIA

Buko-vina

Alsace-Lorraine

FRANCE

AUSTRIA

HUNGARY

ROMANIA

SWITZERLAND

South Tyrol

Slovenia

ITALY

YUGOSLAVIA

BULGARIA

Dalmatia

Bosnia-Herze-govina

Adriatic Sea

ALBANIA

GREECE

a demilitarised zone; and the Saar, a key coal-mining region, was placed under the new League of Nations' control. In addition, all German colonies became mandates (territories under the trusteeship of the League of Nations), and the Allies insisted that the German government agree to uphold a democratic constitution and allow free elections in its own country.

The Germans were also required to pay substantial financial compensation. The final figure, decided by the Reparations Committee in 1921, was set at £6,600 million, and all the foreign currency and assets of Germany abroad were seized. Not surprisingly, the German government thought the figure too high. To justify reparations, the Allies inserted Article 231 into the treaty ('the war-guilt clause'), which obliged Germany to accept full responsibility for the

PEACE AND FUTURE CANNON FODDER

The Tiger: "Curious! I seem to hear a child weeping!"

A cartoon produced in 1919 by Will Dyson for the *Daily Herald* shows the leaders of Britain, Italy, France and the USA leaving the Versailles peace conference. ('The Tiger' is Georges Clemenceau, the French Premier.) Is this cartoon a fair and accurate commentary on the Versailles treaty?

outbreak of the war. Every German greeted the terms of the Treaty of Versailles with varying degrees of anger, horror and disgust. The German leaders who signed the treaty were branded by nationalists as 'the criminals of 1919'.

It is easy to understand the harsh reaction in Germany to the Treaty of Versailles. Most Germans had little idea of the size of the German defeat, and believed that because Germany had requested an armistice, a lenient settlement would follow. As a result, the Treaty of Versailles came as an enormous shock to them. However, the loss of 13 per cent of German territory was much less harsh than France had suffered at the Congress of Vienna between 1814 and 1815, and was far less punitive than the division of Germany would be after the Second World War; it was certainly mild when compared to terms imposed on Russia by the Treaty of Brest-Litovsk. It is also possible to suggest that the reparations were affordable, if only the German government had really been prepared to reduce German citizens' living standards. In fact, the underlying economic and military potential of Germany remained favourable. Germany was surrounded by a number of weak powers in eastern Europe, and faced no strong military alliance. Its industry was modern, with a high level of skill in areas useful for armaments production. The German army was reduced, but its key strategists remained in office. Germany therefore appeared In an excellent position to pose a threat to Europe again.[5] However, the psychological impact of the Treaty of Versailles on Germany was a much more important factor in subsequent events than such objective assessments. Quite clearly, all Germans considered the treaty to be harsh and blamed it for the social, economic and political ills of the Weimar Republic, which replaced the empire. It is hard to deny that the Treaty of Versailles, whether lenient or otherwise, proved a very crucial rallying point for the revival of German nationalism, while the belief in its harshness also encouraged the British government to follow a policy of appeasement during the inter-war years.

The eastern European and Turkish settlements

The other major treaties decided at Paris, which dealt with the other four defeated Central powers – Austria-Hungary, Bulgaria and Turkey – also aroused criticism. The settlement of the territory of the former Austro-Hungarian Habsburg Empire was the most complex problem that the peacemakers faced. The promise to ensure that principles of national self-determination were applied to the widely diverse ethnic and national groups in central and eastern Europe proved extremely difficult to implement, and few ethnic groups were ever satisfied with the settlement in eastern Europe. The Treaty of Trianon (1920) concerned Hungary, and was arguably even harsher than the Treaty of Versailles. Hungary lost 66 per cent of its territory and 40 per cent of the ethnically diverse population of its former empire. Most former Hungarian terrItory went to Romania, the new republic of Czechoslovakia, and Yugoslavia. The Treaty of St Germain (1919) dealt with Austria. All the former territory of the Habsburg Empire outside Austria was shared between Czechoslovakia, which gained Bohemia and Moravia (including, the

Sudetenland, with a population of 3.5 million German speakers); Italy, which gained South Tyrol; Yugoslavia, which received Slovenia, Bosnia-Herzegovina and Dalmatia; Poland, which gained Galicia; and Romania, which was awarded Bukovina. The desire of Austria to unite with Germany was strictly forbidden. Under the Treaty of Neuilly (1919), Bulgaria lost territory to Yugoslavia and Greece.

To further the principle of national self-determination, the peacemakers created two completely new states: Czechoslovakia and Yugoslavia. The historic state of Poland, carved out of German, Austrian and Russian territory, was also restored, but soon became a virtual military dictatorship. Yugoslavia, formed from Serbia, with the addition of territory from Austria, Hungary and Bulgaria, was bitterly divided between the dominant Serbs and their Croat rivals, and also lurched towards the right politically. Czechoslovakia, fashioned out of Austrian, Hungarian, Russian, Romanian and Polish territory, was the only fully functioning democracy in eastern Europe during the inter-war years. Even so, minority groups in Czechoslovakia claimed that each of the republic's coalition governments was so dominated by the Czechs, who made up 65 per cent of the population, as to render the principle of national self-determination virtually meaningless.[6]

The noble idea of national self-determination did not end traditional ethnic rivalries and disagreements. Eastern Europe was arguably more unstable and divided after the First World War than ever before, and a political vacuum now existed. The successor states of the former Habsburg Empire were weak, politically divided, and in a poor economic condition, with little industry, weak currencies, inefficient agriculture, high debts and low investment. Falling world agricultural prices during the inter-war years ensured that eastern Europe remained impoverished. The trading relations of each eastern European government were stormy, due to the continued use of protective tariffs.

What is more, parliamentary democracy never took root in eastern Europe. Hungary was deeply unstable, and developed its own brand of fascist dictatorship during the 1930s. Austria was a political battleground between right and left until parliamentary government gave way to right-wing dictatorship. Bulgaria and Romania also developed right-wing dictatorships, led by their respective kings. Even among the three new states of eastern Europe – Czechoslovakia, Yugoslavia and Poland – democracy was not in the ascendancy.

The foreign relations of these eastern European states were also tense. The Hungarian government disliked Czechoslovakia, Romania and Yugoslavia; the latter three powers responded by forming a close alliance in 1921 – known as the 'Little Entente'. Polish–Czech relations were also hostile, and Yugoslavia and Romania disliked each other intensely. To add to the tension, the Soviet Union was locked in bitter territorial disputes with Poland and Romania, and the German government refused to accept the settlement of its former territory in eastern Europe. The only country in Europe which actively supported the new successor states was France, which signed treaties of mutual assistance with Poland (1921), Czechoslovakia (1924), Romania (1926) and Yugoslavia (1927). The French government hoped that this group of eastern European powers, all of which were committed to upholding the peace settlement in eastern Europe, might provide stability in the region. Yet these states, with their divided loyalties, and discontented ethnic minorities, were no compensation to France for the loss of the Franco-Russian alliance.[7]

The settlement of the territory of the former Ottoman Empire also produced tension and uncertainty. The Treaty of Sèvres (1920) divided Turkey into British, French and Italian spheres of influence, and placed all former Ottoman possessions under British and French administration. However, a Turkish nationalist group (the 'Young Turks') gained power and chose to fight rather than to accept the peace terms. The matter was only finally resolved, after further haggling and small-scale military engagements, by the Treaty of Lausanne (1923), under which Turkey accepted its loss of colonies in return for a guarantee of territorial integrity.

The non-European settlement

The way in which the peacemakers dealt with the settlement of non-European problems left a great deal to be desired. A demand by Japan to have a clause proclaiming a commitment to 'racial equality' placed in the covenant of the League of Nations was rejected. National groups who demanded the right to self-determination in the Middle East, Africa and India were politely informed that the principle would not apply to them. In fact, imperial rule was actually expanded at the Paris Peace Conference. All former Turkish and German colonies were termed 'mandated territories' and placed under the supervision of the victorious powers. The British Empire assumed control of the former Ottoman territories of Palestine, Iraq and Transjordan, as well as the former German African colonies of Togoland and the Cameroons. The French gained control over Syria and Libya, and were allowed access to oil in Mosul. The fig leaf of a League of Nations mandate hid old-fashioned imperial gains; British and French officials claimed that they were marching the mandated territories towards independence, but nationalist groups doubted if such a day would ever arrive.

The disposal of the former German colonies in the Asian–Pacific region served only to inflame relations between China and Japan still further. China had entered the war on the side of the Allies in 1917, and as a result expected to regain control of former German colonies on the principle of national self-determination. However, Japan, an ally of Britain since 1902, had seized these areas in 1914, and now expected to retain them. The peacemakers decided that Japan would keep its trading rights in Manchuria and Inner Mongolia, but would not gain political control of these areas. It was also decided that Japan should supervise the administration of Shantung, provided that it promised to return the area to China at a future date. This settlement satisfied neither Japan nor China, and laid the basis for a long-running and bitter dispute between the two nations, which eventually led to full-scale war in 1937.

The League of Nations and the limits of international co-operation, 1919–33

As well as working out a post-war settlement, the Paris Peace Conference also gave birth to the League of Nations, which was designed to create a completely new framework of international relations. The league had an agreed constitution, outlined in its covenant, which pledged to 'respect and preserve against external aggression the territorial integrity and existing political independence of all members of the league', and to 'take action against any member regarded as an aggressor' through economic sanctions, and if these failed, through 'collective military action'. The organisation consisted of an assembly, which met annually; a council, which had regular meetings and four permanent seats (held by Britain, Italy, France, Japan), raised to five with the addition of Germany in 1926, and four temporary seats, elected by the assembly, raised to six in 1926, and to nine in 1929. It was in the council that the real power lay, but as each member had a veto, there was not much real power to exercise. The day-to-day administration of the league was carried out by the secretariat. The Permanent Court of International Justice was also established at The Hague, to offer 'advisory opinions' on questions referred to it by the assembly or the council.

The League of Nations was a loose and flexible organisation, whose members pledged to uphold an agreed set of principles set out in the covenant. It faced a number of problems in establishing its authority. Defeated powers were denied entry until they proved a willingness to abide by the treaties imposed upon them. The original members were the 32 Allied powers and 12 additional neutral states. 'A victors' club' was how the league was viewed in Germany; 'a capitalist club' was how the Soviet Union, also denied entry, described the new organisation. But the biggest blow of all to the early credibility of the league was the decision of the US Senate, driven by internal political motivations, to block US entry. This deprived the league of both one of its key architects, and of the most powerful non-European power. In reality, the league was largely a European club, dominated by the victorious powers. Very few European diplomats thought that the League of Nations would replace the self-interests of each nation state.

During the 1920s, the league enjoyed mixed success as an effective peacekeeper. On the one hand, a number of minor disputes were settled by the league, most notably the withdrawal of Yugoslavian troops from Albania, and the resolution of a territorial dispute over the Åland Islands between Finland and Sweden. Successful arbitration was achieved in disputes between Germany and Poland over Upper Silesia; between Britain and Turkey over the administration of oilfields in Mosul; and between Greece and Bulgaria over disputed territory in the Balkans. On the other hand, the league could not prevent Poland from annexing Vilna in 1922, Italy from occupying Corfu in 1923, or stop the war between Bolivia and Paraguay in the early 1930s. An even more worrying development was its complete failure to implement the

Geneva Protocol, which had been designed to commit all league members to engagement in collective military action in the event of acts of unprovoked aggression. France was a keen supporter of the idea, but it was vetoed by Austen Chamberlain, the British foreign secretary, in March 1925. The British believed that the Geneva Protocol would turn the league into a 'policeman of the world', and would involve Britain in all manner of minor and major disputes.

However, the League of Nations did promote a greater level of international co-operation than had ever existed before. This climate encouraged the signing by Britain, Japan, France and the USA of the Washington Naval Agreement in 1922, which agreed to limits on naval shipbuilding, and the 1930 London Naval Agreement, signed by Britain, Japan, Italy and the USA, which set limits on submarines and provided for the scrapping of some warships. This same spirit encouraged the signing by 15 major powers in August 1928 of the Kellogg–Briand Pact, which pledged all its signatories to reject 'war as an instrument of national policy', and promised to settle disputes between nations by 'pacific means'. By 1933, 60 nations had made this pledge, very much in the spirit of the covenant of the League of Nations.

The World Disarmament Conference

The biggest disappointment of the league during this period was its total failure to achieve a reduction in armaments on land. The World Disarmament Conference, organised by the league, opened in 1932, and was attended by 61 nations and five non-members, including the USA and the Soviet Union. The chief aim was to set agreed limits on army, air-force and naval weapons. A French idea for a League of Nations army was rejected. A second proposal by the British government to place limits on 'offensive' weapons, including tanks, bomber aircraft, submarines, poison gas and chemical weapons, also floundered. More alarmingly, the German and Soviet delegations refused to accept a resolution passed by 41 votes to prohibit air attacks, the use of tanks and chemical weapons. The German delegation constantly argued for 'equality of rights', and demanded either that the other powers disarm to the German level imposed at Versailles, or that they should allow Germany to rearm to the level of the other major powers. Frustrated, in 1932 the German delegation walked out of the conference and agreed only to return if Germany was given equal treatment.[8] In October 1933, Germany would also leave the League of Nations.

The 'German problem' during the 1920s

The political climate of the Weimar Republic

The dominant issue during the 1920s remained the 'German problem'. Every European statesman agreed that peace could only really be secured if Germany could be reconciled to accepting the terms of the Treaty of Versailles. However, Germany, though still potentially a great power, emerged from the

First World War in a deeply unstable condition. The Weimar Republic (named after the town where its new constitution was agreed), was born in a climate of defeat, national humiliation, chaos, revolution and disorder. Its constitution contained deep flaws: Article 48 gave the president the power to rule without parliamentary support in an emergency; the voting system was organised on the basis of proportional representation, which both encouraged the growth of unstable coalition governments, and allowed all manner of cranks a voice in the Reichstag. Most coalitions depended on the Social Democratic Party (SPD), representing moderate labour interests; the Catholic Centre Party (*Zentrum*), a religious-interest party; and the *Deutsche Volkspartei* (DVP), the representative of industry. Many political parties opposed democracy, including the Communist Party (KPD) and the Independent Social Democrats (USPD), both of whom agitated for a Marxist revolution. On the extreme right were a plethora of nationalist and ultra-right-wing groups, which desired an overthrow of the republic and its replacement by a military dictatorship.[9]

Political instability, with no party ever commanding an overall majority in the Reichstag, was a feature of the precarious political life of the new republic. The infant republic's survival depended greatly on the loyalty of the army, which prevented several attempts to overthrow the government in its early years, including the left-wing Spartacist revolt in 1919 and the Kapp Putsch, led by nationalists in the army in 1920. Out on the mean streets of Weimar Germany, every night was all right for fighting. Left- and right-wing paramilitary groups engaged in pitched street battles, often resulting in many deaths and hundreds injured. This added to the prevailing feeling of instability and gloom.

The 'great inflation' and reparations

In such deeply unstable conditions, any economic upheaval was bound to create problems. Severe financial crises, which most Germans blamed on Allied demands for reparations, were another fact of life during the Weimar years. In recent times, historians have shown that the immediate post-war economic crisis in Germany was largely the result of extensive government borrowing during the war, undertaken on the assumption that Germany would win the war, and that its enemies would pay off its loans. From 1918 to 1923 the German mark went into free fall, and inflation rose into the stratosphere. In 1920, the mark was worth 10 per cent of its 1914 value; by 1922, a mere 1 per cent; and in January 1923, one pre-1914 gold mark would have been worth 2,500 paper marks. It is difficult to ignore the possibility that the German government quite deliberately engineered the 'great inflation', or, at the very least, was not unhappy with its consequences. After all, the eventual collapse of the mark solved the problem of Germany's war and industrial debts, and gave the German government a convincing reason not to pay reparations. The image of ordinary Germans taking wheelbarrows full of money along to their local shop to buy a loaf of bread provoked sympathy around the world. For ordinary Germans, with savings and pensions, however, the 'great inflation' was a disaster which heated a simmering cauldron of discontent among the normally stolid German middle classes (*Mittelstand*).

The German government was able to blame the 'great inflation' on the demand by the Allies for reparations, which, in 1921, were finally set at the seemingly astronomical figure of £6,600 million. Germany's battle over the payment of reparations was undoubtedly the most dominant issue of international affairs during the 1920s.[10] Germans saw the reparations bill as a symbol of everything they hated about the Versailles Treaty, while the French saw reparations as being vital to their own economic recovery; the British government increasingly adopted a central position. The hard approach of France, and the soft approach of Britain, towards the German problem put great strain on Anglo-French relations during the early 1920s.

The German government was able to exploit these Anglo-French divisions in order to win concessions. For example, as inflation rose in Germany from 1921 onwards, the British urged France to agree to a temporary postponement of reparations. However, Raymond Poincaré, who became French prime minister in January 1922, ignored this advice, and, when Germany defaulted on payments in November 1922, he decided to occupy the Ruhr (a major German industrial region) and Belgium, which French troops did in January 1923. This action annoyed the British government, which refused to support it; in response to the occupation of the Ruhr, the German government supported a programme of 'passive resistance'. The occupation of the Ruhr was a major political blunder by Poincaré, who was replaced as prime minister by Edouard Herriot, who adopted a more conciliatory line. The whole episode showed that France alone, acting without British support, could never hope to force Germany to pay reparations. Equally, the German government realised that a policy of continual non-payment was unlikely to produce any meaningful concessions. In these circumstances, the USA was called upon to act as a mediator between Germany and France over the reparations problem. In 1924, an Allied committee, chaired by Charles G. Dawes and Owen D. Young, two leading American bankers, examined Germany's ability to pay reparations, and produced a set of measures designed to aid the German economic recovery. This new atmosphere resulted in the end of the French occupation of the Ruhr. A new German mark, guaranteed by German land and industry, ended the era of hyperinflation, and stimulated recovery.

The Dawes Plan and the Treaty of Locarno

Greatly influenced by Gustav Stresemann, German chancellor between 1923 and 1924 and foreign secretary between 1924 and 1929, the German government accepted that the best way in which to revise the Versailles Treaty during a period of German military weakness was to co-operate with the Allies.[11] This conciliatory approach quickly produced results. In April 1924, the Dawes Committee submitted its proposals, which were agreed at the London Reparations Conference of July–August 1924. Under the Dawes Plan, Germany agreed to make regular annual payments in return for a substantial loan raised in the USA, and the French promised never again to use force to gain payment. The greatest symbol of Stresemann's conciliatory approach during the mid-1920s was the Treaty of Locarno. Under this agreement, signed in 1925 by Britain, France, Germany and Italy, Germany agreed to accept the terms regarding its western frontiers that had been decided at Versailles, including the permanent demilitarisation of the Rhineland. In return, Germany won an immediate end to the Allied military occupation of the Rhineland city of Cologne, a promise of an early end to the occupation of the Rhineland (this took place in 1930), and the end of Allied inspection of the German military. Germany also agreed to join the League of Nations. In recognition of their efforts to make peace, Stresemann, Briand (the French foreign minister) and Austen Chamberlain were jointly awarded the Nobel Prize for Peace.

It seemed that the Treaty of Locarno had laid the basis for a real and lasting solution to the 'German problem'. Germany seemed to be on a path of peace and reconciliation with the rest of Europe. However, this was perhaps an overoptimistic assessment. The German government may have accepted Germany's western frontiers, but it offered no similar commitments to respect its eastern frontiers. In fact, Stresemann and leading officials of the German foreign office saw Locarno, along with the Dawes Plan, as being key stages on the road to a complete revision of the Treaty of Versailles. The Dawes Plan gave Germany important access to US loans with which to pay reparations, and a pool of new investment for German industry. Germany received far more in US loans from 1924 to 1929 than it ever paid in reparations. In 1929, the Young Plan revised the German reparations bill to a quarter of its original total.

It is also important to assess the underlying aims of Stresemann's conciliatory approach to foreign policy during the late 1920s. Stresemann privately believed that the great tasks of future German policy were threefold: to end reparations completely; to liberate Germany from all occupying forces; and in future to gain the 'readjustment of our eastern frontiers'.[12] This would involve the *Anschluss* (the union of Germany and Austria), the recovery of Danzig, the 'Polish Corridor' (the land which divided Germany and East Prussia), and a correction of the frontier of Upper Silesia. Thus, it would appear that Stresemann's foreign policy was double-edged – he seemed to be a peacemaker and a 'good European' in public, but in private he was a German nationalist who cherished the long-term objectives of recovering German territory in eastern Europe. This is not to suggest that Stresemann was a 'Nazi in a pin-striped suit', but it does illustrate how deeply the desire for a wholesale revision of the Treaty of Versailles ran through all sections of German society. On the other hand, Stresemann can be viewed as wanting international respectability for Germany, and its restoration to equal status amongst the great powers, rather than as setting in motion plans for vast territorial expansion along the lines of imperial Germany.

The threat to German democracy: Adolf Hitler and the Nazi Party

The period from 1924 to 1929 is often portrayed as the 'golden age' of the Weimar Republic. German democracy seemed secure, the economy was showing promising signs of recovery, and reparations were no longer causing Franco-German antagonism. However, trouble was bubbling under the surface: the German economic recovery was dependent on US loans; bitterness between the political left and right continued; and many members of the middle class still harboured deep anger over the economic losses that they had suffered during the 'great inflation'. Another worrying sign for the future political stability of the Weimar Republic was the election of Paul von Hindenburg, a hero of Kaiser Wilhelm's army, as president in 1925.[13] Democracy in Germany was now dependent on an unstable coalition between the SPD, the Centre Party and the DVP, and on an ageing and reactionary president who had little love for democracy.

An even bigger potential danger to Weimar democracy was also lurking in the undergrowth. His name was Adolf Hitler, and his personality and objectives are so crucial in understanding the origins of the Second World War that they must be examined in some detail.[14] Hitler was born on 20 April 1889 in Braunau-am-Inn, Austria, near the Austrian–German border. His father was a relatively affluent customs official, his mother a 'traditional housewife'. The family soon moved to Linz, where the young Adolf attended private, fee-paying schools. After the death of both his parents, and an inglorious school career, Hitler moved to Vienna in 1907, where he hoped to become 'a great artist' and tried unsuccessfully to gain entry to the prestigious Academy of Arts. Contrary to popular myth, Hitler was never really down-and-out in Vienna, but he was certainly going nowhere. He was unemployed – by choice – and lived for nearly three years on a substantial legacy, left to him in his mother's will, until it ran out. He visited the opera regularly, and mostly hung out in local cafés, eating chocolate cake, drinking endless cups of coffee, and voicing his exceedingly large number of prejudices and hates to anyone who would listen. From 1910 to 1913 he lived in a hostel for the homeless and, by 1912, he was earning some money selling his drawings and paintings. In 1913, Hitler fled across the border into Germany to avoid being conscripted into the Austrian army. When the First World War began, Hitler was in Munich, the capital of Bavaria, where he volunteered to join the German army. Hitler had found his two great loves – the army and war. He served with distinction, being twice awarded the Iron Cross for bravery, and being promoted to the rank of lance corporal. For most of the time, he was a motorcycle messenger between the Western Front and the headquarters of the German army.

On the day that news came of the German defeat, Hitler was in hospital, recovering from a poison-gas attack. He was utterly devastated and could not believe it. In July 1919, when Hitler heard the terms of the Treaty of Versailles, he decided to enter politics. His dream was to build a 'new Germany' under his own leadership, to overturn the Treaty of Versailles, and to establish Germany

influenced by the Depression. Political instability in China threatened Japanese trading interests in the region and, when coupled with the Depression, these two factors prompted the army to opt for formal Japanese rule of Manchuria. On 18 September 1931, an explosion on the railway line of the South Manchurian Railway, near Mukden, took place. This was instigated by Japanese army officers, but was blamed on Chinese nationalists, and provided an ideal excuse for Japan to justify its occupation of Manchuria.

China called on the League of Nations for help, but the league did not consider imposing either economic or military sanctions on Japan. The British government, which had substantial imperial interests in the region, was too preoccupied with its own economic problems to press for military action. The US government offered mild words of protest, but took no action. It was actually the Japanese government which requested the League of Nations to examine the facts of the case. A League of Nations commission, headed by Lord Lytton, concluded that Japanese claims to the region were convincing, but rebuked Japan for using force in support of them. Japan ignored this mild scolding, stayed in Manchuria, and left the League of Nations in 1933.[18] The failure of the League of Nations to act effectively during the Manchurian Crisis is often viewed as the beginning of the slide towards international anarchy during the 1930s, but there is little contemporary evidence to confirm this view. The Manchurian Crisis was greeted with a great deal of indifference, and cannot be convincingly linked to later events in Europe, even though the Sino-Japanese dispute over Manchuria remained a key source of instability in the Asian-Pacific region.

Hitler's rise to power

It is generally agreed that the most acute effects of the Great Depression were felt in Germany. From 1925 to 1929, Germany paid £5,000 million in reparations, but received £9,000 million in US loans. As soon as these loans dried up, the German economy collapsed. Unemployment stood at 1.4 million in 1928, but had soared to 6 million by 1932. Industrial production fell by 42 per cent, and agricultural prices collapsed. The political effects were equally catastrophic: the fragile centre coalition of the SDP, DVP and the Centre Party fell from power in March 1930. From March 1930 until January 1933, when Hitler came to power, Germany was in effect under a veiled dictatorship, with each chancellor ruling with the consent of President von Hindenburg, under Article 48 of the constitution, and with no majority in the Reichstag.

In March 1930, von Hindenburg appointed Heinrich Brüning, a member of the Centre Party, chancellor of a so-called 'national' government, which introduced a bleak set of deflationary policies, including tax increases, pay reductions, redundancies, and harsh public-expenditure cuts. This pushed the Germany economy further into decline, and increased unemployment. In a desperate attempt to win his regime some popular legitimacy, Brüning called a general election in September 1930. At the election, Hitler's Nazi Party benefited from a remarkable surge of popular support, increasing its seats in the Reichstag from 12 to 107, raising its votes from 810,000 to 6.5 million, and emerging as the second-largest party, behind the SPD.

The German election of 1930 provided Hitler with an ideal opportunity to play on the anxiety of German voters in the midst of the Depression. Hitler regarded the political and economic chaos of Weimar Germany with the 'greatest glee', and believed that 'the eyes of the German people have been finally opened to the unimaginable lies, trickeries and deceits of the Marxist traitors of the nation'. On 13 October 1930, the 107 Nazi deputies (members of the Reichstag), dressed in their brown shirts, entered the Reichstag. Toni Sender, a socialist member, later described what he saw that day: 'I looked at their faces carefully. The more I studied them, the more I was terrified by what I saw: so many with the faces of criminals and degenerates. What a degradation to sit in the same place with such a gang.'[19]

The election had been a total failure for Brüning, who went on ruling by emergency decree, and searched for a foreign-policy success with which to divert the public's attention from the worsening state of the German economy. In March 1931, Brüning proposed an 'economic *Anschluss*' with Austria, through the formation of a customs union. The French government protested, and the International Court of International Justice at The Hague declared the proposal illegal. French bankers withdrew money from the Austrian Credit Anstalt Bank, which collapsed, followed by two major German banks. Under such financial pressure, the humiliated Brüning was forced to withdraw his proposal. Brüning's next high-handed move in foreign affairs was unilaterally to stop German reparations payments in 1932, but this move was accepted by the Allies (who finally ended the programme of reparations at Lausanne in 1932).

Throughout 1932, Germany was gripped by the fear of either a Nazi or a communist dictatorship, or a return to high inflation. Speculation was rife in the German press that Hitler would shortly come to power. Many doubted this would happen: for example, the communist Ernst Thälmann, the KPD leader, told a friend on the day before Hitler actually came to power: 'The bourgeoisie won't let Hitler anywhere near power. Let's go to Lichtenberg and play skittles.'[20] On 13 March 1932, Hitler challenged von Hindenburg in the presidential election. In order to obstruct Hitler's campaign, Brüning banned his paramilitary storm-troopers (the SA), while the SPD, the Centre Party and liberals urged voters to support von Hindenburg. To everyone's relief, von Hindenburg defeated Hitler by 19 to 13 million votes. Even so, the election established Hitler as the second most popular leader in Germany, and sealed the fate of Brüning, whose ban of the SA was opposed by the army. It now seemed that either a military dictatorship, led by an army figure, or a 'Hitler cabinet' were the only two options left to von Hindenburg. He finally decided to appoint the relatively unknown Franz von Papen, a wealthy Catholic aristocrat from Prussia, chancellor of a 'cabinet of barons' with clear authoritarian policies. Von Papen immediately declared a state of emergency, suspended the Prussian parliament (the last stronghold of the SPD), lifted the ban on Hitler's SA, and called a national election.

In the election of 31 July 1932, the Nazis enjoyed another sharp surge of support. They won 230 seats and 37.4 per cent of the popular vote. This made the Nazi Party the largest parliamentary group ever to sit in the Reichstag. The pressure was now mounting on von Hindenburg to invite Hitler to form a government by presidential decree. In 1932, the Nazi Party had united the conservative and nationalist right-wing factions of German politics, and dominated rural and small-town Germany, while also making gains in certain affluent, middle-class districts. On the whole, the increase in support for Hitler from 1930 to 1932 came from groups which had been hit by the Depression – white-collar workers, small shopkeepers, old-age pensioners, self-employed workers, civil servants, teachers, skilled artisans working in small businesses, and young university students. Despite all the subsequent research on the subject, it is probably still correct to view the rise of Nazism as a revolt of the German middle class who had been hit by the Depression.

Although the von Papen regime had no majority in the Reichstag, it remained in power, primarily because von Hindenburg wanted to exhaust all the other right-wing possibilities before turning to Hitler. After the election, von Papen said that 'the system of parliamentary democracy has broken down and is incapable of resurrection'.[21] He openly acted like a 'Nazi in a pin-striped suit' by raising tariffs on British goods by 300 per cent; informing the World Disarmament Conference of Germany's intention to rearm; demanding the return of German colonies and the Saar; and staging a military parade of 180,000 war veterans in a clear throwback to Germany's imperial days. All this did nothing to improve his precarious political position. In October 1932, a vote of no confidence in his government in the Reichstag was passed by 512 votes to 42.

This triggered yet another election on 6 November 1932, in which Nazi support surprisingly dropped from 230 to 196 seats, and fell by 2 million votes. The election revealed that Nazi support was on the wane, but it also showed that popular support for von Papen was non-existent, and he was forced to resign. Rumours now spread about what type of regime would replace von Papen's. It was clear that von Hindenburg wanted some sort of right-wing, authoritarian regime, but no one was quite sure if this meant a return of the Kaiser, now in exile, an army dictatorship, or a right-wing coalition led by Hitler. Von Hindenburg finally decided on an army dictatorship led by General von Schleicher, who became chancellor in December 1932, but he lasted a mere 57 days. On 30 January 1933, von Hindenburg abruptly dismissed him, and finally decided to appoint Hitler chancellor in a right-wing coalition government which contained only three Nazis. Von Hindenburg was persuaded by von Papen to give Hitler the post of German chancellor in the hope that this might restrain the Nazi leader. However, the appointment of Hitler as German chancellor abruptly ended all the illusions that the 'German problem' had been solved.

The Paris Peace Settlement

3.1 Clemenceau outlines the French position towards Germany at the Paris Peace Conference

Report of the 'Council of Four' meeting, 27 March 1919

I said yesterday that I entirely agreed with Mr David Lloyd George and President Wilson on how Germany should be treated; we cannot take unfair advantage of our victory; we must deal tolerably with peoples for fear of provoking a surge of national feeling . . . Mr Lloyd George has excessive fears of possible German resistance and refusal to sign the treaty . . . They will dispute on every point, they will threaten to refuse to sign . . . they will contest or refuse everything that can be refused . . . President Wilson warns us against giving the Germans a sense of injustice. Agreed, but what we regard as just here in this room will not necessarily be accepted as such by the Germans . . . Shortly before he died Napoleon said: 'Nothing permanent is founded on force.' I am not so sure; a glance at the great nations of Europe is enough to give one pause. What is true, is that force cannot establish anything unless it is in the service of justice. Every effort must be made to be just towards the Germans; but when it comes to persuading them that we are just to them, that is another matter. We can, I believe, save the world from German aggression; but the German spirit is not going to change so fast.

Source: A. Adamthwaite, *The lost peace: international relations in Europe, 1918–39*, London, 1980, pp. 24–27

3.2 Hitler's view of the Versailles Treaty

Written in Mein Kampf

When in the year 1919 the German people was burdened with the peace treaty, we should have been justified in hoping that precisely through this instrument of boundless repression the cry for German freedom would have been immensely promoted. Peace treaties whose demands are a scourge to nations not seldom strike the first roll of drums for the uprising to come . . . We had to form a front against this treaty and engrave ourselves forever in the minds of men as an enemy of this treaty, so that later, when the harsh reality of this treacherous frippery would be revealed in its naked hate, the recollection of our attitude at that time would win us confidence.

Source: A. Hitler, 'The diktat of Versailles', in I. Lederer (ed.), *The Versailles settlement: was it foredoomed to failure? The truth about the treaty*, London, 1960, pp. 86–90

3.3 The economic consequences of the peace: a British view

John Maynard Keynes' view

The treaty is no treaty, because it is now generally recognised that in truth it settles nothing . . . If you pledge a man to perform the impossible, you are no nearer a decision as to what in fact he has to do: for his pledge is, necessarily a dead letter. The reparations clauses of this treaty are its most important economic feature. But being composed of foolish, idle words, having no relation to real facts, they are without practical effect, and they leave the prospects of the future undetermined . . . This treaty ignores the economic solidarity of Europe, and by aiming at the economic life of Germany it threatens the health and prosperity of the Allies themselves . . . by making demands the execution of which is in the literal sense impossible, it stultifies itself and leaves Europe more unsettled than it found it.

Source: J. M. Keynes, *The economic consequences of the peace*, London, 1920

3.4 Reparations against Germany: an American view

The opinion of an American delegate at the Paris Peace Conference

The magnitude of the reparations demanded of Germany under the treaty . . . placed great strain upon credit. Largely on this account there was a widespread collapse of the entire pre-war system of goods and services and investments. The pre-war gold system has collapsed and a large part of the world functions in terms of closed international dealings restricted to barter . . . The reparations clauses contributed largely toward a German psychology which has changed the political complexion of much of the world.

Source: J. F. Dulles, 'Foreword', in P. Burnett, *Reparations at the Paris Peace Conference*, New York, 1940

3.5 The Paris Peace Settlement: a communist view

From a contemporary communist pamphlet

The imperialist war of 1914 demonstrated with the greatest clarity to all enslaved nations and oppressed classes of the entire world the falseness of bourgeois-democratic phraseology. Both sides used the phrases of national liberation and the right of national self-determination to make good their case, but the treaties of Brest-Litovsk and Bucharest on one side, and the treaties of Versailles and St Germain on the other, showed that the victorious bourgeoisie quite ruthlessly determine 'national' frontiers in accordance with their economic interests . . . The so-called League of Nations is nothing but the insurance contract by which the victors of war mutually guarantee each other's spoils . . . The League of Nations and the entire post-war policy of the imperialist states discloses this truth even more sharply and clearly, everywhere intensifying the struggle of the proletariat of the advanced countries and of the labouring classes in the colonies, accelerating the destruction of petty-bourgeois national illusions about the possibility of peaceful coexistence and of the equality of nations under capitalism.

Source: A. Adamthwaite, *The lost peace: international relations in Europe, 1918–39*, London, 1980, pp. 39–41

3.6 The Paris Peace Settlement: a British assessment

The view of a British delegate at the Paris Peace Conference

The historian, with every justification, will come to the conclusion that we were very stupid men. I think we were . . . We came to Paris confident that the new world order was about to be established; we left it convinced the new order had fouled the old . . . We arrived determined that a peace of justice and wisdom should be negotiated: we left it conscious that the treaties imposed were neither just nor wise . . . It is impossible to read German criticism without deriving the impression that the Paris Peace Conference was guilty of disguising an imperialist peace under the surface of Wilsonism . . . Hypocrisy was the predominant and inescapable result . . . We had accepted a system for others which, when it came to practice, we should refuse to apply to ourselves.

Source: H. Nicolson, *Peacemaking 1919*, New York, 1939

Document case-study questions

1 Identify the major criticisms made of the Treaty of Versailles by John Maynard Keynes in 3.3.

2 What does 3.2 tell us about Hitler's reaction to the treaty?

3 How far did the Treaty of Versailles reflect Clemenceau's views as outlined in 3.1?

4 Comment on the way in which the League of Nations is dealt with in 3.5.

5 According to 3.4, what is the major weakness of the Treaty of Versailles?

6 To what extent does Nicolson's assessment in 3.6 conform to your own view of the peace settlement?

7 Evaluate the strengths and weaknesses of all the above documents as historical sources.

Notes and references

1 Quoted in A. Adamthwaite, *The making of the Second World War*, London, 1977, p. 36.

2 J. Joll, *Europe since 1870*, London, 1973, pp. 196–238; P. M. Kennedy, *The rise and fall of the great powers*, London, 1988, pp. 330–54.

3 There is extensive literature on the Paris Peace Settlement. Historians whose works take a sympathetic view include A. Adamthwaite, *The lost peace: international relations, 1918–39*, London, 1980; R. Henig, *Versailles and after, 1919–33*, London, 1984; G. Ross, *The great powers and the decline of the European states system, 1914–45*, London, 1983; and M. Trachtenberg, 'Versailles after sixty years', *Journal of Contemporary History*, vol. 16 (1982). For critical accounts, see E. H. Carr, *International relations between the wars, 1919–39*, London, 1948; S. Marks, *The illusion of peace: international relations in Europe, 1918–33*, London, 1979; and A. J. P. Taylor, *The origins of the Second World War*, London, 1961.

4 P. Mantoux, *Paris Peace Conference, 1919: proceedings of the Council of Four*, Geneva, 1964, pp. 24–29.

5 A. Lentin, *The Versailles Peace Conference: peacemaking with Germany*, London, 1991.

6 For details of the treaties, see J. Grenville (ed.), *The major international treaties, 1914–73*, London, 1974.

7 A. Polonsky, *The little dictators: the history of eastern Europe since 1918*, London, 1975.

8 See R. Henig (ed.), *The League of Nations*, Edinburgh, 1973.

9 There is a vast body of literature on the Weimar Republic. The following studies are useful: R. Bessel and E. J. Feuchtwanger (eds.), *Social change and political development in Weimar Germany*, London, 1981; E. Eyck, *A history of the Weimar Republic*, 2 vols., Oxford, 1962, 1964; and I. Kershaw (ed.), *Weimar: why did German democracy fail?*, London, 1990.

10 E. Bennett, *Germany and the diplomacy of the financial crisis*, Harvard, 1962.

11 H. A. Turner, *Gustav Stresemann and the politics of the Weimar Republic*, Princeton, 1963.

12 Quoted in E. Sutton (ed.), *Gustav Stresemann: his diaries, letters and papers*, London, 1937, pp. 503–5.

13 See A. Dorpalan, *Hindenburg and the Weimar Republic*, Princeton, 1964.

14 See A. Bullock, *Hitler: a study in tyranny*, London, 1962; J. Fest, *Hitler*, London, 1977.

15 The classic study of Hitler's rise during the Weimar period is A. J. Nicholls, *Weimar and the rise of Hitler*, London, 1968. A very good recent study is C. Fischer, *The rise of the Nazis*, Manchester, 1995.

16 For a detailed discussion of Nazi voters, see T. Childers, *The Nazi voter*, London, 1983.

17 C. Kindelberger, *The world in depression, 1929–39*, London, 1973.

18 A. Iriye, *The origins of the Second World War in Asia and the Pacific*, London, 1987, pp. 6–33.

19 Quoted in J. Toland, *Adolf Hitler*, New York, 1976, p. 333.

20 Quoted in D. Smith, *Left and right in twentieth-century Europe*, London, 1970, p. 32.

21 *Time Magazine*, 19 September 1932.

4 The origins of the Second World War: 2 From peace to global war, 1933–41

The impact of Hitler

The period from 1933 to 1941 was one of deep international instability, which eventually resulted in the Second World War. The tension began with the appointment of Adolf Hitler as German chancellor in January 1933. This immediately raised deep concerns that Germany would soon rearm and openly challenge the Paris Peace Settlement. However, Hitler was initially too concerned with consolidating Nazi control over Germany to take a great interest in foreign affairs. During 1933, the books of 'unsuitable' writers were burned, civil rights were suspended, opposition parties and trade unions were banned, and the democratic press was closed down. Jews were excluded from public office, Hitler's political opponents were arrested, beaten up and sent to concentration camps, and the Nazi swastika was used as the national flag. The cruelty of the Nazi regime led to a wave of moral indignation and demonstrations in many countries: a wax model of Hitler in Madame Tussaud's museum in London was daubed in red paint with the words 'Hitler the Murderer'; anti-Nazi parades were held in several major US cities; and a petition signed by 228 Jewish organisations in the USA called on President Roosevelt to institute a boycott of German goods.

In the face of this foreign opposition, Hitler decided to proceed cautiously in the realm of foreign affairs, and repeatedly made soothing speeches which insisted that Germany wanted peace. At the World Disarmament Conference, Hitler suggested that all the other major powers either disarm to match the German level of armaments set at Versailles, or that they allow Germany to rearm to the same level as all the other major powers. Ramsay MacDonald, the British prime minister, urged the French to accept this request, but they would only agree if Germany, as an act of good faith, accepted the Versailles arms limits for another four years. In October 1933, Hitler withdrew Germany from both the World Disarmament Conference and the League of Nations on the grounds that neither would treat Germany on equal terms.[1]

These moves provoked fears about Nazi intentions. To ease these worries, Hitler signed a non-aggression pact with Poland in January 1934. The Polish government thought that the agreement offered them security against Soviet ambitions, but it seems that Hitler signed the agreement to thwart a possible

Franco-Polish alliance, and to bring Poland under German influence. The agreement was viewed by the British press as a sign of Hitler's peaceful intentions, but the French were more suspicious and, in April 1934, the French government announced that it would 'henceforth assure her [France's] security by her own means'. Meanwhile, the arrival of Hitler on the international scene allowed the Soviet Union to emerge from years of diplomatic isolation. In November 1933 the USA officially recognised the Soviet Union and restored diplomatic relations. In July 1934, the Soviet Union was admitted to the League of Nations.

However, the summer of 1934 featured a series of events which once more fixed world attention on Nazi Germany. Rumours spread that Hitler was about to engineer the *Anschluss* (the union of Austria with Germany). Dollfuss, the Austrian chancellor, opposed the idea, and in June 1934 slapped a ban on the Austrian Nazi Party. A month later, he was assassinated by pro-Nazi extremists. This action provoked world-wide outrage: Mussolini, the Fascist leader of Italy, sent four army divisions to the Austrian border, and the French and Italian governments issued a joint declaration opposing any attempt to undermine Austrian independence. Hitler was forced to deny any German involvement in the murder of Dollfuss, and refuted any Nazi plan for an armed seizure of Austria.[2]

Meanwhile, a crisis erupted in domestic German politics which shocked most liberal-minded people in the democracies. Hitler ordered a lawless and merciless eradication of his political rivals (during the 'night of the long knives' between 29 and 30 June 1934): General von Schleicher, the former German chancellor; Gregor Strasser, a leading socialist figure in the Nazi Party; and Ernst Röhm, leader of the SA, were among those brutally murdered. On 2 August 1934, President von Hindenburg, the last link with any vestige of the Weimar era, died peacefully at his home in Neudeck. This greatly strengthened Hitler's power in Germany: he swiftly abolished the post of president, ended the Weimar constitution, and declared himself *Führer* ('Leader') of the German people. Each member of the German armed forces was now required to swear a personal oath of allegiance to Hitler – not the state.

The early months of 1935 witnessed a number of major developments in international affairs. In January 1935, 90 per cent of voters in the Saar region of Germany, in a plebiscite held by the League of Nations, opted for the restoration of the area to Germany. In the same month, France and Italy signed a diplomatic agreement which resolved mutual discord in North Africa, and promised co-operation in the event of German aggression. On 16 March 1935, the Nazi propaganda ministry assembled the world's press to announce what everyone already knew: Germany was rearming. The German army was now 400,000 strong (the Treaty of Versailles had limited it to 100,000), conscription was introduced, the air force and navy were undergoing rapid programmes of expansion, and Hitler claimed that Germany was no longer bound by the military clauses of the Treaty of Versailles. This announcement caused public outrage. Britain, France and Italy met at Stresa in April 1935, and issued a joint declaration which opposed 'by all practical means any unilateral repudiation of treaties which may endanger the peace of Europe', and asserted Austrian independence. The 'Stresa Front' seemed to be a great public show of unity against German revisionism regarding the terms imposed at Versailles, but in reality it pronounced empty rhetoric. No action was taken against Germany.

In May 1935, in a speech designed to ease British, French and Italian fears, Hitler said: 'Germany needs peace and desires peace.' He also promised not to interfere with his 'beloved Austria' and proposed disarmament agreements. *The Times* wrote of 'Hitler's sincerity and peaceful intentions', but the French government thought otherwise, and signed a pact with the Soviet Union under which each side offered assistance to the other in the event of an unprovoked attack by Germany. France and the Soviet Union also signed an agreement to protect Czechoslovakia from a German attack. The British government, which deeply mistrusted the Soviet Union, was unhappy with these French moves, and decided to make a significant gesture of appeasement towards Nazi Germany by signing an Anglo-German naval agreement in June 1935 which limited German shipbuilding to a level of 35 per cent of that of the Royal Navy. This was little hardship for Nazi Germany, as it would take years to reach the set limit. The agreement was a diplomatic triumph for Hitler, because it recognised Germany's right to rearm, and also revealed the hollowness of the Stresa Front.[3]

The collapse of the League of Nations, 1935–37

In October 1935, Italy suddenly invaded Abyssinia (modern-day Ethiopia), the last independent nation state in Africa.[4] This was the first unprovoked attack by any European power since the establishment of the League of Nations, but it was not completely unexpected: Italy had long sought to avenge its Italian defeat by Abyssinia at Adowa in 1896. News of the attack broke during the 1935 British general-election campaign. Stanley Baldwin, the prime minister and leader of the Conservative Party, who was fighting his campaign under the slogan 'peace with collective security', was placed in the embarrassing position of being forced to make a public show of opposition towards this demonstration of unprovoked aggression. Samuel Hoare, the British foreign secretary, asked the League of Nations to impose economic sanctions on Italy. These were imposed, but proved ineffective, because many countries were not league members and because oil, a key war material, was not included in the sanctions.

The French government did not want to punish Mussolini too harshly: it regarded Italy as a vital counterweight to German designs on Austria. Hoare decided to meet Laval, the French foreign minister, in Paris, to try to find a way of easing the pressure on Italy. Hoare and Laval privately agreed to Italy gaining most of Abyssinia, except for a small strip of land along the coast (later dubbed by *The Times* 'a corridor for camels'). When it was leaked to the press, the Hoare–Laval Pact caused deep political embarrassment. After all, Hoare and Laval were condoning Italian aggression in private, while condemning it in public. Hoare was forced to resign. The whole Abyssinian affair was a disaster for Britain and France. It showed that they only paid lip-service to the ideals of the League of Nations, it destroyed the Franco-Italian alliance, and it alienated Mussolini.[5]

The next of Hitler's surprises came on 7 March 1936, when German troops marched into the demilitarised Rhineland. The French government offered words of outrage, but decided that it would not use force to reverse Hitler's action.[6] Anthony Eden, the British foreign secretary, claimed that British policy was designed 'to come to peaceful agreed solutions by appeasement of justified grievances', and although he pledged British support of France in the event of a German attack, he claimed that the occupation of the Rhineland had to be accepted as an accomplished fact. The view of *The Times* that Hitler was only 'going into his own back garden' became widely accepted. By marching his troops into the Rhineland, Hitler had removed a key grievance created by the Treaty of Versailles, and was now in an excellent geographical position to launch an attack on France. The League of Nations took no action and ceased to have any significant influence on the subsequent course of events.

The outbreak of the Spanish Civil War in October 1936 added to the sense of anarchy in international relations. The war grew out of the circumstances surrounding the collapse of yet another fragile democracy. In February 1936, Nationalists became the largest group in the Cortes (Spanish parliament), but a Popular Front coalition, consisting of republicans, socialists and communists, combined to prevent them from taking power. The Nationalists, led by General Franco, who had commanded the Spanish army in Morocco, refused to accept this decision and set up an alternative government, supported by the army. A civil war was soon under way to decide who should rule Spain. The Nationalists presented the civil war as an ideological struggle between fascism and communism, while the Popular Front viewed the war as a battle between democracy and fascism. The issues dividing both sides were very complicated, and produced deep rifts. Hitler and Mussolini provided military support to Franco, Stalin helped the Popular Front, but the British and French decided on a policy of non-intervention, not wishing to inflame the likely winner. Despite all the fears that the Spanish Civil War raised about an impending European war, it remained a local conflict which ended in a victory for Franco by early 1939. The Spanish Civil War was a notable success for Germany and Italy in their ideological battle with communism. The victory of Franco also allowed Germany and Italy easy access to a range of important war materials, including iron ore, copper, zinc, tin and mercury.[7]

The year of 1936 was one of enormous success for Hitler's Nazi Germany. In July, Austria agreed to accept the supervision of its foreign policy by Germany in return for a guarantee regarding its sovereignty. In August, the Nazis were praised for the organisation of the Olympic Games, held in Berlin. In the same month, Hitler announced a new four-year plan, which aimed to increase the domestic production of vital raw materials, including synthetic rubber, fuel oil and iron ore, and brought industry more directly into the service of the aims of the Nazi Party. In October, Hitler and Mussolini signed the Rome–Berlin Axis, in which they loosely agreed on collaboration, which illustrated the movement of Italy away from Britain and France. In November, Germany and Japan signed the Anti-Comintern Pact, which promised joint action to prevent the spread of communism, and which raised the spectre of a possible alliance between Germany, Italy and Japan. By the end of 1936, the German economy had dramatically recovered, unemployment was virtually eradicated, rearmament was pushed forward at a rapid rate, and Hitler's popularity stood at an all-time high.[8]

The US response to the growing turmoil in Europe was complex. Franklin D. Roosevelt, the US president, had private worries about the threat posed by Nazi Germany to world peace, and was often willing to condemn acts of aggression by Germany, Italy and Japan. However, the key aim of his foreign policy was to keep the US out of any future war. The prevailing US attitude towards Nazi Germany up to the time of the Munich Conference in 1938 was to support the appeasement of legitimate German grievances. For example, when Hitler marched into the Rhineland, the French government urged the US government to condemn the action, but Roosevelt remained silent. A powerful isolationist group in the US Congress passed a series of neutrality acts in the 1930s, designed to ensure that the USA would remain on the sidelines in any future war.[9] As Neville Chamberlain, who became the British prime minister in 1937, put it: 'It is always best and safest to count on nothing from Americans except words.'

In the Far East, Japan was also posing a threat to peace. Spending on national defence in Japan grew from 31 per cent of GDP in 1931 to 47 per cent in 1936. In the summer of 1936, the Japanese government, now increasingly dominated by the army, promulgated the 'fundamentals of future national policy', which defined the Asian-Pacific region as Japan's 'sphere of influence', and promised the gradual expansion of Japanese interests in Southeast Asia. What is more, the Japanese government refused to renew the Washington and London naval agreements which limited Japan's naval expansion. In July 1937, the poor relations between China and Japan turned into open war. Japanese troops swiftly advanced along the coastal ports of China, but soon became bogged down. The Chinese government called on the League of Nations for help. The league proposed an international conference of major powers in Brussels, but no military help was offered. Britain and the US did provide financial assistance to China, but the war dragged on.

Neville Chamberlain, appeasement and the road to Munich, 1937–38

Appeasement and the alternatives

It was pretty clear by 1937 that international relations were in a state of turmoil. Germany and Italy were threatening peace in Europe, Japan was at war with China, and a bitter civil war was under way in Spain. It was against this background that Neville Chamberlain, aged 68, became the British prime minister. He was a dull figure, with the appearance of a bank manager. In his case, however, appearances were misleading. Chamberlain was a man with a mission, who wanted to bring order and lasting peace to international relations through a policy known as 'appeasement'. The task of explaining why appeasement became the policy adopted by the British government to meet the deepening crisis of the 1930s is complex. Any consideration of the reasons for appeasement must mention several factors.

1 There was a widespread horror at the idea of a second world war.
2 Too much faith had been placed in the League of Nations, which proved ineffective when faced with military aggression.
3 There was a widespread feeling that Germany had been punished too harshly by the Treaty of Versailles.
4 British public opinion constantly opposed the rearmament of Britain.

Furthermore, the position of France, Britain's only firm ally, had sharply deteriorated in the face of the growing fascist threat. The Locarno Treaty, designed to protect France from attack, had been ignored by Germany, the Franco–Italian agreement had broken down, and Belgium had opted for neutrality. The German army was moving into a position of superiority, while the Spanish Civil War had raised the prospect of another hostile power over the French border. In such circumstances, the French government had no desire to go to war, and was increasingly looking to Britain to provide a new direction in Franco-British relations with Nazi Germany and Italy. Finally, the poor state of Britain's armed forces also influenced the policy of appeasement and often justified it. Britain was in no position to offer any help to France, either to defend its cities from air attack, or to defend its possessions in the Far East from Japan.

The policy of appeasement grew out of an intermingling of all these factors. This is not to suggest that it was inevitable, but in the difficult circumstances of international affairs in the late 1930s it seemed rational and logical to Chamberlain. It was not, however, the only policy available. There were two alternative directions which British foreign policy could have taken in the late 1930s. The first was to support peace by collective security through the League of Nations, but this policy had never been implemented, even when the league was strong, and stood less chance of success in 1937, when the league was weak and discredited. A second alternative was to create a 'grand alliance' of the anti-fascist powers, a policy championed by Winston Churchill, who suggested that the dictators would only respond to military force. Yet this policy amounted to a return to the pre-1914 alliance system, and very few leaders like to adopt a past policy which has already proved unsuccessful, even though in this case it might have prevented war.

The only other option was to satisfy the grievances created by the Paris Peace Settlement, and Chamberlain, along with the majority of the 'National

Government', favoured this stance. A bold policy of appeasement came to be seen by Chamberlain as the only choice if war was to be avoided. He believed that unless he could negotiate a revision of the Treaty of Versailles with Hitler, then a second world war would probably break out.[10]

The sudden desire of Chamberlain to champion appeasement as an active policy with which to solve the grievances of Nazi Germany was not appreciated by Hitler. In May 1937, for example, Chamberlain invited von Neurath, the German foreign minister, to the coronation of George VI, but Hitler refused to let him go, on account of the negative coverage of Nazi Germany in some British newspapers. In November 1937, Chamberlain sent Lord Halifax, a kindred spirit, to meet leading Nazi figures, much to the annoyance of Sir Anthony Eden, the foreign secretary, who felt that Chamberlain's attempt to court the dictator might end in failure. At his meeting with Hitler, Halifax said that Britain would support any legitimate German claims in Europe, provided they were negotiated peacefully.

The Hossbach Memorandum

However, Hitler treated the Halifax visit as an unwelcome intrusion into his own military plans. On 5 November 1937, Hitler summoned von Neurath, General von Blomberg, the war minister, and other leading military chiefs to a meeting to discuss his future plans. A record of the meeting was kept by Colonel Hossbach, from memory, which later became known as the 'Hossbach Memorandum'. In the document, which most historians accept as being authentic, Hitler suggested that the key aim of German policy was 'conquest in the east', which had to be achieved by some time between 1943 and 1945 while Germany still held a clear military lead over Britain and France. Hitler also told the meeting that Austria and Czechoslovakia had to be seized, and predicted that these actions might provoke a war with France and Britain.[11] Shortly after the conference, Hitler started to remove moderate members of the 'old guard' from key positions. In November 1937, Schacht, the economics minister who opposed the rapid pace of rearmament, was dismissed. In January 1938, von Blomberg was also dismissed; Hitler became minister of war, and new, pro-Nazi men were moved into the other leading positions. Von Ribbentrop, a key Nazi, replaced the moderate von Neurath as foreign minister.

The *Anschluss*

During 1938, Hitler's actions brought Europe to the brink of war. In January 1938, the Austrian police discovered Nazi plans for a seizure of power in Austria, even though Hitler had no plans at that time for an invasion. Alarmed by this discovery, Schuschnigg, the Austrian leader, met Hitler at Berchtesgaden, Hitler's mountain retreat, on 12 February 1938. At the meeting, Hitler bullied Schuschnigg into signing an agreement which brought two Nazis into the Austrian cabinet, allowed Nazis complete freedom in Austria, and gave Germany total control of Austrian foreign policy. On his return to Austria, however, Schuschnigg – quite bravely – decided to call a referendum which asked voters to support a 'free and independent Austria'. It was a provocative move designed to gain popular support to resist German aggression. When the vote seemed likely to reject union with Germany, Hitler bullied and threatened Schuschnigg once more, and he was forced to resign. A new, Nazi-dominated Austrian government, led by Seyss-Inquart, invited Germany to occupy Austria. On 12 March 1938, German troops entered Austria, with Hitler driving through the packed streets of Vienna in triumph. The *Anschluss* had been achieved by bullying and intimidation, but without a single shot being fired.[12]

The response of Britain and France to the *Anschluss* was predictable. On the very day on which Hitler's troops marched into Austria, France was without a government. The French eventually uttered strong words of protest, but there was no question of military action. Neville Henderson, the British ambassador in Berlin, laid most of the blame on Schuschnigg for calling the referendum. As a result of the *Anschluss*, the Treaty of Versailles was virtually destroyed, the balance of power in central Europe turned sharply in Germany's favour, and the position of Czechoslovakia was now under grave threat.

The Czech crisis of 1938

Czechoslovakia consisted of a number of mixed nationalities artificially amalgamated into a nation state by the peacemakers of Versailles. Hitler called Czechoslovakia a dagger thrust into the heart of Germany. Yet Czechoslovakia was the only democracy left in central Europe, led by the highly respected Edvard Beneš, who had played a significant role in the work of the League of Nations. Within its borders lived the 3.5 million German speakers of the Sudetenland. Since 1933 Hitler had given financial support to the pro-Nazi Sudeten German Party, led by Konrad Henlein. During the remainder of 1938, Hitler cast himself as the defender of this so-called 'oppressed minority' of Sudeten Germans. The Czech crisis was made even more complicated by the existence of a Franco-Czech alliance dating back to 1925, and the Franco-Soviet Pact of 1935, which both promised to preserve the integrity of Czechoslovakia. This meant that the Czech crisis held the prospect of turning into a European war.[13] However, France had no wish to go to war to save Czechoslovakia, and the Franco-Soviet Pact only became operative if France acted first.

Chamberlain believed that the Czech problem had to be solved by negotiation. In May 1938, the Czech government claimed that Germany was ready to invade. France, the Soviet Union and Britain all promised aid to Czechoslovakia in the event of a Nazi assault. A very angry Hitler was forced to deny that any German plans for an invasion existed. Yet when the 'May crisis' died down, Hitler set a firm date for a German invasion of Czechoslovakia – 1 October 1938. Chamberlain decided that the British government should act as a mediator between the Sudeten Germans and the Czech government. To this end, Lord Runciman, the Liberal leader in the House of Lords, who had no reputation as a conciliator, was sent to Czechoslovakia in August 1938 to try and find a settlement to the problem. The Czech government offered every possible concession, but the Sudeten German Party, encouraged by Hitler, kept asking for more, and the negotiations broke down. In his report, Runciman depicted the Sudeten Germans as an oppressed minority, and advised Chamberlain to allow them to join Hitler's Third Reich.

By September 1938, the crisis was mounting. Hitler whipped his supporters into a frenzy at the Nuremberg rally by claiming that the Sudeten Germans were 'not defenceless and not alone'. At this point, Chamberlain made his boldest move, travelling by aeroplane to meet Hitler, in order to find out what the Nazi leader wanted and to try to give it to him. The French government stayed on the sidelines. Hitler met Chamberlain at Berchtesgaden on 15 September 1938, and told Chamberlain that Germany wanted the Sudetenland to be incorporated into the Third Reich. On 21 September 1938, the Czech government was given a stark choice by the British and French governments: agree to a peaceful handover of the Sudetenland to Germany, or fight alone. Under this extreme pressure, the Czechs reluctantly agreed to the former.

Chamberlain, the self-styled 'messenger of peace', took this news to Hitler at Bad Godesberg on 22 September 1938, but he then found that Hitler had new demands, which included an immediate German occupation of the Sudetenland, with those Czechs who wished to leave only being permitted to take a single suitcase of belongings with them. Astonishingly, Chamberlain was even willing to agree to this. However, the British cabinet, the Czech government and the French government could not. War now seemed likely. 'How horrible, fantastic, incredible it is', said Chamberlain in a live broadcast on BBC radio on 27 September 1938, 'that we should be trying on gas masks here because of a quarrel in a far-away country between people of whom we know nothing.'[14]

It was left to Mussolini, who was in no position to go to war, to persuade Hitler to settle the matter peacefully at Munich. Hitler (for Germany), Chamberlain (for Britain), Daladier (for France) and Mussolini (for Italy) met on 29 September 1938 to decide the fate of Czechoslovakia. The Munich Conference was a return to old-fashioned European diplomacy, with four major European powers forcing a small nation to concede territory. It was justified on the principle that national self-determination had been denied to the Sudeten Germans in the first place. The Munich Conference simply agreed to the Sudetenland being incorporated into Germany by 10 October 1938. A vague promise to respect the integrity of the rest of Czechoslovakia was given by the four powers. It seems that Hitler, despite gaining the Sudetenland without firing a shot, was dissatisfied with Munich and was eager to push ahead with his own desire to occupy the remainder of Czechoslovakia at the earliest opportunity. In a separate meeting, Chamberlain persuaded Hitler to sign a piece of paper which declared that Britain and Germany would 'never go to war with one another again'. To Hitler, it was a worthless piece of paper, but Chamberlain flourished it on his return to Heston airport from Munich. This gesture would haunt him to his dying day.[15]

Nevertheless, the Munich agreement, despite its dubious morality, did solve a major German grievance without a major European war. It was heralded as a triumph for Chamberlain's bold new policy, and he was nominated for the Nobel Peace Prize for 1938. President Roosevelt sent him a telegram with the simple message 'good man'. Not everyone agreed: Winston Churchill described the events at Munich as the 'blackest page in British history'; the Soviet Union believed that Britain and France were happy so long as Hitler moved eastward. The seeds of the later Nazi–Soviet Pact were probably planted in the mind of the Soviet leader, Stalin, at the time of Munich. As for Hitler, he said, as he celebrated yet another bloodless triumph: 'With a dictator nothing succeeds like success.' The Czech crisis, which went on for over six months, was a traumatic experience. The cheers and acclaim for Chamberlain were symbolic of a deep longing to avoid a second world war.

The road to global war, 1938–41

These optimistic hopes of a lasting peace in Europe did not last very long. On 9 November 1938, groups of Nazi thugs toured the Jewish areas of every town and city in Germany, and engaged in an orgy of violence and thuggery which included smashing shop windows, burning synagogues and beating up ordinary Jewish people. *Kristallnacht* (the 'night of broken glass') sent a wave of shock throughout the world. President Roosevelt denounced the Nazi attack on German Jews as an act which he thought 'could not happen in the twentieth century'. An opinion poll showed that 70 per cent of the British public were horrified by the attack and wanted no further negotiations with Nazi Germany; Lord Mount Temple, president of the Anglo-German Fellowship, resigned in protest; the House of Commons voted unanimously to condemn the action. The morality of negotiating with such an obviously brutal regime was now called into question. In the early months of 1939, a number of voices were raised against the policy of appeasement: Lloyd George suggested that appeasement was a policy which 'lacked courage'; Duncan Sandys, Churchill's son-in-law, and Basil Liddell Hart, the military correspondent of *The Times*, formed the 'Hundred Thousand Party', which pledged to fight Chamberlain's appeasement of Hitler; and the Federation of University Conservatives passed a resolution against appeasement. In January, following intelligence reports from Germany which indicated a possible German attack on Holland, pressure grew on Chamberlain within the cabinet to make a greater public commitment towards the defence of western Europe. On 6 February, Chamberlain announced that Britain would support France in the event of any threat to its vital interests anywhere. This amounted to an Anglo-French alliance. This decision was followed by the creation of a large British Expeditionary Force pledged to fight to save France in the event of war and by the opening of staff talks between British and French army chiefs of staff.

On 15 March 1939, Germany occupied the remainder of Czechoslovakia, Bohemia and Moravia. Hitler claimed that he was 'invited in to restore order', but no one was convinced. The British and French governments claimed that because the Czech government fell before the German occupation, the guarantee offered at Munich did not apply. However, British, French and US public opinion was deeply outraged. Chamberlain was forced, by the strength of public opinion, to assume a position of anger and indignation towards Nazi Germany. On 17 March, in a speech made in Birmingham, Chamberlain asked if the German occupation of the Czech capital city, Prague, was the 'last attack on a small nation? Or is it to be followed by others? Are the aggressions of Germany a step in the direction of an attempt to dominate the world by

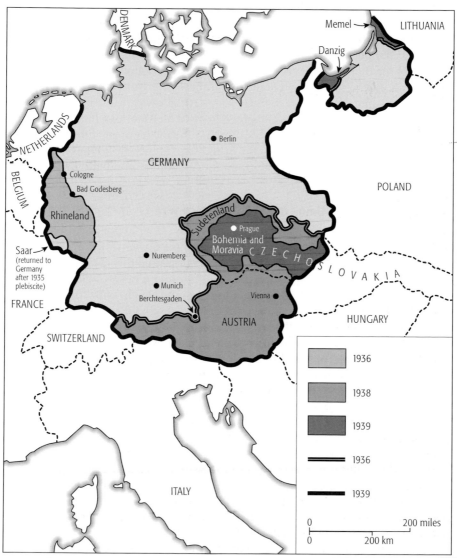

Map 5. The territorial expansion of Nazi Germany, 1936–39.

force?'[16] The German occupation of Czechoslovakia crushed all hopes that Hitler could be appeased by concessions. It was now pretty clear that Hitler was out to dominate Europe by force. Roosevelt denounced Hitler's invasion as an act of 'wanton lawlessness', recalled the US ambassador to Czechoslovakia, and slapped a 25 per cent tax on all German goods. All Czech funds in London and French banks were frozen. Daladier, the French prime minister, put France on a virtual war footing.

Any hope that these actions would halt Hitler's aggression were quickly disappointed. On 21 March 1939, Hitler seized Memel, on the border of East Prussia and Lithuania, and asked Poland to return the free city of Danzig to Germany. On 31 March, Britain and France agreed to give a unilateral guarantee of support to Poland in the event of an unprovoked attack on it.[17] This new change of policy seemed to have little impact on the aggressive designs of the dictators, however, and on 7 April Mussolini seized Albania. On 13 April, further British and French guarantees were offered to Romania, Greece and Turkey; 'a guarantee a day keeps Hitler away' ran a popular joke of the time. On 15 April, Roosevelt agreed to send an American battle fleet from the Atlantic to the Pacific, to counterbalance the Japanese naval threat in the region, and to thereby allow the British and French fleets to return to Europe. The British government also announced conscription into their armies for all men aged 20 and 21.

The role of the Soviet Union in the outbreak of war

In April 1939, Churchill said that the guarantee system did not go far enough, and urged Chamberlain to seek an alliance with the Soviet Union. The vast majority of British and French public opinion supported this idea. But, Chamberlain, a lifelong anti-communist, had profound misgivings about concluding an Anglo-Soviet alliance. In the end, the weight of British public opinion forced him to make a half-hearted attempt to gain an Anglo-Soviet agreement.[18] Chamberlain believed an alliance with the Soviet Union would arouse the suspicion of Poland and aggravate the hostility of Hitler. It was the gravity of the international situation, and the strength of public opinion, which forced him to change course. In June 1939, a public opinion poll showed 84% of British people were in favour of an Anglo-Soviet alliance. In these circumstances, Chamberlain, very reluctantly and with little real enthusiasm, agreed to open negotiations with the Soviet Union in the summer of 1939. Sir Anthony Eden offered to lead the negotiations, but Chamberlain turned down this request. The diplomatic talks were conducted by Sir William Strang, a low-ranking foreign office official, and proved very slow and complex. The British military mission to the Soviet Union was headed by a virtually unknown naval figure with a name as long-winded as the negotiations: Admiral Sir Reginald Aylmer Ranfurly Plunket-Ernle-Erle Drax. He did not depart for the Soviet Union until 5 August – no doubt delayed while filling out his visa application. Drax journeyed to Moscow by a merchant ship which took six days to arrive. The talks were cordial, but they broke down on 19 August

A cartoon for the London *Evening Standard* drawn by David Low in 1936. Evaluate the cartoonist's presentation of Hitler's foreign policy.

primarily because the Polish government steadfastly refused to allow Soviet troops to enter Polish territory in the event of war. However, the generally low-key approach to the discussions by the British government was probably a fatal blunder which paved the way for the Nazi–Soviet Pact.

In the summer of 1939, the Soviet Union, ignored, isolated and mistrusted for most of the inter-war period, was now at the centre of European diplomacy. Everyone assumed, especially Chamberlain, that Hitler's hostility to Soviet communism was so passionate that he would never contemplate a Nazi–Soviet pact. This view ignored Hitler's opportunism and his willingness to be flexible in pursuit of his foreign-policy aims. Hitler had already set 1 September 1939 as the date for the invasion of Poland, and knew that the Soviet Union was the only power which could offer any real assistance to Poland. With these considerations in mind, Hitler sent von Ribbentrop, the German foreign minister, to meet Stalin to conclude a pact with the Soviet Union. On 23 August 1939, the Nazi–Soviet Pact was signed. Hitler saw the pact as a temporary measure, designed to frighten Britain and France out of their guarantee to Poland. For his part, Stalin was as indifferent to the fate of Poland as Chamberlain had been towards Czechoslovakia a year earlier, and wanted to keep the Soviet Union out of a war with Nazi Germany if at all possible.[19]

The outbreak of war in Europe

In the final days of August 1939, Hitler assumed that Britain and France would not go to war to save Poland. On 29 August 1939, Hitler offered the Poles the opportunity to agree to his demands by negotiation, but the Polish government refused. Chamberlain had offered a guarantee to a small nation which was quite willing to undertake a suicidal war with Nazi Germany, and was prepared to drag Britain and France along with it. On 1 September 1939, Germany attacked Poland. On 3 September 1939, Britain and France declared war on Germany. Italy decided to remain neutral, and the participants in the European war which began in September 1939 were confined to Germany, Poland, Britain and France. However, as Britain and France stood on the defensive in western Europe, for the time being it was really a German–Polish war. Poland was predictably crushed in less than five weeks. The start of the elimination of Jewish people in Poland began almost immediately.

The first nine months of the Second World War were dubbed the 'phoney war', as hardly a shot was fired by Britain and France against Germany. More British people died in the blackout (when city lights were extinguished as a precaution against bombing raids) during this period than on the battlefield. In April 1940, Denmark was occupied by Germany without resistance. The first time that Britain and France engaged German troops was in Norway, and they were fairly soundly defeated. In May 1940, Germany launched its major attack on western Europe. Holland and Belgium fell quickly. The French, supported by the British army, which was eventually evacuated from France at Dunkirk, were crushed by the Nazi *Blitzkrieg* in less than six weeks. At this point, Mussolini, believing that Germany had already won the European war, finally entered on Hitler's side. The Nazis occupied Paris and the French government moved to Vichy, to begin years of humiliating collaboration with Germany. By the end of 1940, most of Europe was under Nazi rule. In September 1940, a Tripartite Pact was signed between Germany, Italy and Japan. Hitler stood at the pinnacle of his power.

In May 1940, Churchill had replaced Chamberlain as prime minister of Britain. From May 1940 until June 1941, Britain stood alone, survived the aerial Battle of Britain in the summer of 1940, and hoped for a miracle. It came in June 1941, when Germany suddenly, but not unexpectedly, attacked the Soviet Union. This extended the scale of the European war. The attack on the Soviet Union stands out as Hitler's most carefully calculated plan of his entire period as German leader. The Nazi attack on the Soviet Union does seem to have been a burning desire of Hitler, which he could not resist once he had conquered most of western Europe.

Despite all Roosevelt's strong words against the Axis powers of Germany, Italy and Japan, the USA still remained a spectator to these incredible events. In 1941, however, Roosevelt began to believe that the USA had to prevent the domination of Europe and the Far East by the Axis nations. To help the British, the US offered a scheme entitled Lend-Lease, by which arms were supplied to Britain by lease, sale or exchange. In the summer of 1941, the US banned oil supplies to Japan. This was a highly provocative move, which Roosevelt knew might provoke Japan into war. As the Japanese war effort in China depended on oil imports, two stark choices now faced Japan's leaders – to accept the US demands, or to seize oil supplies by advancing against British, French and Dutch possessions in Southeast Asia.

On the morning of 7 December 1941, Japan launched its famous surprise attack on the US fleet at anchor at Pearl Harbour in Hawaii. President Roosevelt described the attack – which sunk, damaged or destroyed eight US battleships, three cruisers, three destroyers, and 188 aircraft – as a 'day that will live in infamy'. The USA now entered what had become a truly global conflict. On hearing the news of the US entry into the war, Churchill rejoiced, and later said that from that day onwards, 'Hitler's fate was sealed. Mussolini's fate was sealed. As for the Japanese, they would be ground to powder. All the rest was merely the proper application of overwhelming force.'

The Second World War, which ended in 1945, resulted in an overwhelming victory for the Western Allies and in utter defeat for Germany, Italy and Japan. It was the most bloody and devastating conflict in the history of the world. We should never forget the suffering of its victims, and we should never cease to discuss the reasons why it happened.

Document case study

The approach of war

4.1 Hitler's view of the chief aims of future German foreign policy, 1925

From his book, Mein Kampf

We National Socialists must hold unflinchingly to our aim in foreign policy, namely to secure for the German people the land and soil to which they are entitled on this earth . . . State boundaries are made by man and changed by man. The fact that a nation has succeeded in acquiring an undue amount of soil constitutes no higher obligation that it should recognised eternally. At most it proves the strength of the conquerors and the weakness of the nations. And in this case, right lies in strength alone . . . The old German policy was wrongly determined by dynastic considerations, and the future policy must not be directed by cosmopolitan folksy drivel. In particular, we are not constables guarding the well-known 'poor little nations', but soldiers of our own nation . . . But we National Socialists must go further . . . Germany will either be a world power or there will be no Germany . . . And so we National Socialists consciously draw a line beneath the foreign-policy tendency of our pre-war period. We take up where we broke off 600 years ago. We stop the endless German movement to the south and west, and turn our gaze towards the land of the east. At long last we break off the colonial and commercial policy of the pre-war period and shift to the soil policy of the future . . . If we speak of soil in Europe today, we can primarily have in mind only Russia and her vassal border states.

Source: A. Hitler, *Mein Kampf*, translated by R. Mannheim, London, 1969, pp. 596–98

4.2 President Roosevelt on international anarchy, 1937

The 'Quarantine Speech', by President F. D. Roosevelt, Chicago, USA, 5 October 1937

The political situation in the world, which of late has been growing progressively worse, is such as to cause grave concern and anxiety to all peoples and nations who wish to live in peace and amity with their neighbours . . . Without a declaration of war and without warning or justification of any kind, civilians, including women and children, are being ruthlessly murdered with bombs from the air. In times of so-called peace ships are being attacked and sunk by submarines without cause or notice. Nations are fomenting and taking sides in civil warfare in nations that have never done them any harm . . . The peace-loving nations must make a concerted effort in opposition to those violations of treaties, and those ignoring of humane instincts which are today creating a state of international anarchy and instability from which there is no escape through mere isolation or neutrality . . . There can be no stability or peace either within nations or between nations except under laws and moral standards adhered to by all. International anarchy destroys every foundation for peace. It is my determination to pursue a policy of peace and to adopt every practicable measure to avoid involvement in war. We are determined to keep out of war, yet we cannot insure ourselves against the disastrous effects of war and the dangers of involvement . . . America hates war. America hopes for peace. Therefore, America actively engages in a search for peace.

Source: R. Challener (ed.), *From isolation to containment, 1921–52: three decades of American foreign policy from Harding to Truman*, London, 1970, pp. 50–52

4.3 The Hossbach Memorandum, 1937

Minutes of a conference held in the German Chancellery, taken by Colonel Hossbach, Berlin, 5 November 1937

The *Führer* began by stating that the subject of the present conference was of such importance that its discussion would, in other countries, certainly be a matter for a full cabinet meeting . . . He wished to explain to the gentlemen present his basic ideas concerning the opportunities for the development of our position in the field of foreign affairs . . .The aim of German policy was to secure and preserve the racial community (*Volksmasse*) and to enlarge it. It was therefore a question of space . . . German policy had to reckon with two hate-inspired antagonists, Britain and France, to whom a German colossus in the centre of Europe was a thorn in the flesh, and both countries were opposed to any further strengthening of Germany's position either in Europe or overseas . . . Germany's problem could only be decided by force and this carried attendant risk . . . If the *Führer* was still living it was his unalterable resolve to solve Germany's problem of space at the latest by 1943–45 . . . For the improvement of our politico-military position our first objective, in the event of our being embroiled in war, must be to overthrow Czechoslovakia and Austria simultaneously in order to remove the threat to our flank in any possible conflict against the west . . . Actually the *Führer* believed that almost certainly Britain and probably France as well, had tacitly written off the Czechs and were reconciled to the fact that this question would be cleared up in due course by Germany.

Source: *Documents on German foreign policy, 1918–45*, series D, vol. 1, London, 1949, pp. 29–30

4.4 Neville Chamberlain defines his attitude towards Czechoslovakia, 20 March 1938

Excerpt from Chamberlain's diary

You only have to look at the map to see that nothing France or we could do could possibly save Czechoslovakia from being overrun by the Germans, if they wanted to do it. The Austrian frontier is practically open; the great Skoda munitions works are within easy bombing distance of German aerodromes, the railways all pass through German territory, Russia is 100 miles away. Therefore we could not help Czechoslovakia – she would simply be a pretext for going to war with Germany. That we could not think of unless we had a reasonable prospect of being able to beat her to her knees in reasonable time, and of that I see no sign. I have therefore abandoned the idea of giving guarantees to Czechoslovakia, or the French in connection with her obligations to that country.

Source: K. Feiling, *The life of Neville Chamberlain*, London, 1946, pp. 347–48

4.5 The Munich Conference, 1938: an Italian view

Excerpts from the diary of Count Galeazzo Ciano, Italian foreign minister, 29–30 September 1938

29–30 September. In the train the *Duce* ['Leader', Mussolini] is in good humour . . . He criticises British and French policy severely . . . At Kufstein we meet the *Führer*. We get into his carriage, where he spreads out on the table all the maps of the Sudetenland and the western fortifications. He explains the situation: he intends to liquidate Czechoslovakia as she now is . . . The *Duce* listens with concentration. The programme is now fixed: either the conference is successful in a short time or the solution will take place by force of arms. 'Besides', adds the *Führer*, 'the time will come when we shall have to fight side by side against England and France. All the better while the *Duce* and I are at the head of our countries, and still young and full of vigour.' But all that seems superseded by the atmosphere which has been created – an atmosphere of agreement . . . After a brief stop at the palace where the *Duce* and I are staying, we go to the *Führerhaus* [the Leader's house], where the conference will take place. The others have already arrived . . . The *Führer* comes halfway down the stairs to meet us and, with the rest of his suite, singles us, the Italians, by a marked distinction of treatment. Brief, cold handshakes with Daladier and Chamberlain – then the *Duce* goes over to a corner of the room where the Nazi leaders surround him . . . We enter the conference room . . . The *Führer* speaks – a few words of thanks and an exposition of the situation. He speaks calmly, but from time to time he gets excited and then he raises his voice and beats his fist against the palms of his other hand . . . The *Duce* affirms the necessity for a rapid and concrete decision, and with this end in view proposed to use as a basis for discussion a document which has in fact been telephoned to us by our embassy the previous evening, as the expression of the desires of the German government . . . Chamberlain is inclined to linger over legal points. Daladier defends the cause of the Czechs without much conviction, the *Duce* prefers to remain silent and draw conclusions . . . Daladier particularly is loquacious in personal conversations. He says what is happening today is due solely to the pig-headedness of Beneš [the Czech president] . . . At last, at one in the morning, the document is complete. Everybody is satisfied, even the French, even the Czechs, according to what Daladier tells me.

Source: M. Muggeridge (ed.), *Ciano's diary, 1937–38*, London, 1952, pp. 163–68

4.6 Hitler's speech to the generals, August 1939

A speech made prior to Germany's occupation of Poland

[The] decision to attack Poland was arrived at in spring . . . Goering [the head of the air force and the rearmaments programme] has demonstrated to us his four-year plan is a failure and that we are at the end of our strength if we do not achieve victory in a coming war . . . Since the autumn of 1938 and since I realised Japan will not go with us unconditionally and that Mussolini is endangered by that nitwit of a king and the treacherous scoundrel of a crown prince, I decided to go with Stalin . . . As to what the weak western European civilisation asserts about me, that is of no account . . . I experienced those poor worms Daladier and Chamberlain at Munich. They will be too cowardly to attack. They won't go beyond a blockade . . . Poland will be depopulated and settled with Germans. My pact with the Poles was merely conceived as a gaining of time. As for the rest, gentlemen, the fate of Russia will be exactly the same as I am now going through with in the case of Poland. After Stalin's death – he is a very sick man – we will break the Soviet Union. Then will begin the dawn of the German rule of the earth . . . Be hard, be without mercy, act more quickly and brutally than the others. The citizens of western Europe must tremble with horror. That is the most humane way of conducting a war. For it scares the others off.

Source: E. L. Woodward and R. Butler (eds.), *Documents on British foreign policy*, 3rd series, vol. 7, London, 1954, no. 314

4.7 The US oil embargo against Japan, 1941

Memorandum by Sumner Welles, acting secretary of state, of a conversation between Roosevelt and the Japanese ambassador to the USA, 24 July 1941

The president said that for more than two years the United States had been permitting oil to be exported from the United States to Japan. He said this had been done because of a realisation on the part of the United States that if these oil supplies had been shut off or restricted the Japanese government and people would have been furnished with an incentive or pretext for moving down upon the Netherlands East Indies in order to assure themselves of a greater oil supply than that which, under present conditions, they were able to obtain. The United States had been pursuing this policy primarily for the purpose of maintaining peace in the Pacific region . . . The average American citizen could not understand why his government was permitting Japan to be furnished with oil in order that such oil might be utilised by Japan in carrying on her purposes of aggression. The president said if Japan attempted to seize oil supplies by force in the Netherlands East Indies, the Dutch would resist, the British would immediately come to her assistance, and, in view of our policy of assisting Great Britain, an exceedingly serious situation would immediately result.

Source: R. Challener (ed.), *From isolation to containment, 1921–52: three decades of American foreign policy from Harding to Truman*, London, 1970, pp. 58–60

4.8 Japan makes the decision for war

Report of a conference of the imperial Japanese government, 2 July 1941

Agenda: outline of national policies in view of the changing situation

1 Our empire is determined to follow a policy that will result in the establishment of the Greater East Asia Co-Prosperity Sphere and will thereby contribute to world peace no matter what changes may occur in the world situation.
2 Our empire will continue its efforts to effect a settlement of the China incident, and will seek to establish a solid basis for the security and preservation of the nation. This will involve steps to advance south.
3 Our empire is determined to remove all obstacles in order to achieve the above-mentioned objectives.

In order to achieve the above objectives, preparations for war with Great Britain and the United States will be made . . . In carrying out the plans outlined above, our empire will not be deterred by the possibility of being involved in a war with Great Britain and the United States.

Source: I. Nish (ed.), *Japan's decision for war: records of the 1941 policy conferences*, Stanford, 1967, p. 78

4.9 The German invasion of the Soviet Union: the evidence of a German general

Statement of Franz Halder, chief of staff, German army (1938–42), military tribunal, Nuremberg, 22 November 1945

I, Franz Halder, being duly sworn, depose and say as follows:
That, on the first day of April 1938, I took over in the supreme command of the German army, the position of first quartermaster general . . . I, furthermore, state and affirm that in March 1941, before the start of the Russia campaign which happened in June of that year, Hitler called the chiefs of command of the three parts of the armed forces and also high commanders to a conference in the Armed Forces' Chancery . . . In that conference Hitler said as follows: 'The war against Russia will be such that it cannot be conducted in a knightly fashion. This struggle is a struggle of ideologies and racial differences and will have to be conducted with unprecedented, unmerciful and unrelenting harshness. All officers have to rid themselves of obsolete ideologies. I know that the necessity of such means of waging war is beyond the comprehension of you generals, but I cannot change my orders and I insist my orders will be executed without contradiction. The commissars [the heads of Soviet government departments] are the bearers of those ideologies of Russia and are directly opposed to National Socialism. Therefore they, the commissars, will be liquidated. For the German soldiers who are guilty in this fight of breaking international law, provided that breaking of civil law, such as murder, rape or robbery are not involved, then their breach of inter-national law shall be excused. Russia has not participated in the Hague Convention, therefore has no rights under it' . . . When this talk given by Hitler was over, listeners on the part of the army were of course outraged by this speech of Hitler's and some officers turned to Field Marshal von Brauchitsch and gave expressions of feelings

concerning it. Von Brauchitsch then assured them that he was going to fight against this resolution.

Source: *Nazi conspiracy and aggression: a collection of documentary evidence and guide materials prepared by the American and British prosecuting staffs for presentation before the International Military Tribunal at Nuremberg*, 8 vols., vol. 8, Washington DC, 1946–48, pp. 643–47

Document case-study questions

1 Offer an evaluation of the major differences in Hitler's views on foreign policy as expressed in 4.1 and 4.3.

2 Identify the main features of Roosevelt's view in 4.2.

3 Assess briefly the importance of the views expressed by Neville Chamberlain in 4.4.

4 What insights does Ciano provide in 4.5 on the attitudes of Hitler, Mussolini, Chamberlain and Daladier towards the Munich Agreement?

5 What impression of Hitler's aims during the Second World War can be gained from 4.6?

6 In what ways has Roosevelt's attitude towards international problems changed in 4.7 from the views expressed in 4.2?

7 Comment briefly on the significance of 4.8 in establishing primary responsibility for the outbreak of the Asian-Pacific war.

8 What are the strengths and weaknesses of 4.9 as a historical source for explaining the actions of the Germany army during the campaign against the Soviet Union in 1941?

9 Using all the sources, who do you think was responsible for the outbreak of the Second World War?

Notes and references

1 P. Noel-Baker, *The first World Disarmament Conference, 1932–33, and why it failed*, New York, 1979.

2 D. A. Lowe, *The Anschluss movement, 1931–38, and the great powers*, London, 1985.

3 H. H. Hall, 'The origins of the Anglo-German Naval Agreement', *Historical Journal*, vol. 19 (1976).

4 G. Baer, *Test case, Italy, Ethiopia and the League of Nations*, Stanford, 1977.

5 See R. A. C. Parker, 'Great Britain, France and the Ethiopian Crisis', *Historical Journal*, vol. 17 (1974).

6 The most extensive study is C. T. Emmerson, *The Rhineland crisis, 7 March 1936*, London, 1977.

7 There is an extensive body of literature on the Spanish Civil War. The standard work remains H. Thomas, *The Spanish Civil War*, London, 1977.

8 See R. Overy, *The Nazi economic recovery, 1932–38*, London, 1982.

9 The most important studies of US policy in the 1930s are R. Dallek, *Franklin D. Roosevelt and American foreign policy, 1932–45*, Oxford, 1979; and A. Offner, 'The United States and National Socialist Germany', in W. J. Mommsen and L. Kettenacker (eds.), *The fascist challenge and the policy of appeasement*, London, 1983.

10 See D. Dilks, 'We must hope for the best and prepare for the worst', and 'The prime minister, the cabinet and Hitler's Germany, 1937–39', *Proceedings of the British Academy* (1987); F. McDonough 'Why appeasement?' in P. Catterall (ed.), *Britain, 1918–51*, Oxford, 1994; and R. A. C. Parker, *Chamberlain and appeasement: British policy and the coming of the Second World War*, London, 1993.

11 'The Hossbach Memorandum, 10 November 1937', *Documents on German foreign policy, 1918–45*, series D, vol. 1, London, no.19.

12 J. Gehl, *Austria, Germany and the* Anschluss, *1933–38*, Oxford, 1963.

13 See H. Auluch, 'Britain and the Sudeten issue', *Journal of Contemporary History*, vol. 18 (1983).

14 *The Times*, 28 September 1938.

15 There is an extensive debate on the Munich crisis. The most useful contributions include K. Robbins, *Munich, 1938*, London, 1968; P. W. Schroeder, 'Munich and the British tradition', *Historical Journal*, vol. 19 (1976); T. Taylor, *Munich: the price of peace*, London, 1979; and J. Wheeler-Bennett, *Munich: prologue to tragedy*, London, 1948.

16 *The Times*, 18 March 1939.

17 See S. Newman, *March 1939, the British guarantee to Poland: a study in the continuity of British foreign policy*, Oxford, 1976.

18 D. C. Watt, 'The initiation of the negotiations leading to the Nazi–Soviet Pact: a historical problem', in C. Abramsky (ed.), *Essays in honour of E. H. Carr*, London, 1974.

19 G. Roberts, 'The Soviet decision for a pact with Germany', *Soviet Studies*, vol. 44 (1992).

5 The historians and the origins of the Second World War

The changing debate

The Second World War was really two separate wars: a European war and an Asian-Pacific conflict. The historical debate is overwhelmingly dominated by the larger European conflict, but the Asian-Pacific war has also developed a very lively subdebate. The debate on the European war is led by two interpretations. The first suggests that the major cause of the Second World War was Hitler's desire for the expansion of Germany. This view was advanced by prosecution judges who tried leading Nazi war criminals at the international military tribunal held at Nuremberg between 1945 and 1946. The second interpretation concentrates on the policy of appeasement. As Winston Churchill said in 1946, 'There was never a war in all history easier to prevent by timely action than the one which has just desolated great areas of the globe. It could have been prevented without the firing of a single shot, but no one would listen.'[1] The early historical debate portrayed Hitler as the personification of evil and Chamberlain as the epitome of cowardice. The outbreak of the Cold War, which divided the world into US- and Soviet-dominated blocs, did little to remove politics, morality and emotion from the debate.

The views of A. J. P. Taylor

All this helps to explain why A. J. P. Taylor's classic book, entitled *The origins of the Second World War*, had such a profound impact when it was published in 1961. A. J. P. Taylor was known as a dissenter and was famed for supporting controversial positions, but his view of Hitler seemed unbelievable. Taylor claimed that Hitler was not an evil monster who moulded events to fit his master plan, but was a man of 'improvisation', 'opportunism' and 'the spur-of-the-moment bright idea' – 'an ordinary German statesman' whose foreign policy differed little from that of earlier German governments. Taylor put forward an equally controversial view of appeasement, which he saw as being a logical and realistic assessment of the failings of the past, and as being a genuine attempt to solve them. What brought war was not appeasement, but the mistakes that Chamberlain made when he decided to abandon the policy. In Taylor's view, war broke out not because of Hitler's design, but because of Chamberlain's blunders. Hitler's foreign policy succeeded, for a while, because of his ability to seize opportunities and profit from the mistakes of his opponents.[2] These controversial views set the debate on the origins of the Second World War alight, and opened the way to a broader, and less emotionally charged, debate.[3]

The Hitler factor

The orthodox view

Nevertheless, the personality and the foreign-policy aims of Adolf Hitler still dominate the debate. There is abundant evidence indicating that all the major decisions on German foreign policy were taken by Hitler, and equal amounts of evidence showing the confused nature of decision-making within the Third Reich. The debate has developed into a contest between those historians who believe that Hitler had a fanatical will and a consistent programme of aggression, and those who see the Nazi leader as being an unprincipled opportunist, constrained by internal politics, and responding to the ebb and flow of events in a flexible manner.[4] The best-known proponent of the orthodox view of Hitler's foreign policy is Hugh Trevor-Roper (Lord Dacre), who developed the theory of the Nazi leader following a master plan which had been laid out in *Mein Kampf*. The two most persistent themes in Hitler's writings, according to Trevor-Roper, are firstly, a burning desire to gain *Lebensraum* ('living space') in eastern Europe, through a war of conquest against the Soviet Union, and secondly, a passionate determination to find a 'final solution' to the 'Jewish question'.[5] Alan Bullock, the author of the best-known biography of Hitler, also sees a clear consistency in Hitler's views on foreign affairs, but suggests that his pursuit of his long-term goals was combined with opportunism in his method and tactics.[6]

In recent times, the idea of Hitler following a plan in stages has gained widespread support. Andreas Hilgruber suggests that Hitler was following a three-stage plan, which aimed to engage in a war of conquest to dominate Europe, to gain territory in the Middle East, and ultimately to fight a war for global domination with the USA.[7] Klaus Hildebrand suggests a carefully calculated 'stage-by-stage' plan (*Stufenplan*), with the gaining of *Lebensraum* in eastern Europe and the destruction of the Soviet Union as the prerequisites for an eventual war for world domination.[8] Most supporters of these orthodox views see Hitler's foreign policy as a direct outcome of his own clear personal intentions, executed with a high degree of tactical flexibility and improvisation.[9]

The revisionist view

On the opposite side of the debate are the revisionists, who reject the idea of Hitler, as the 'master of the Third Reich', following a unique and deeply personal set of foreign-policy objectives. Karl-Dietrich Bracher suggests that the idea of Hitler being an all-powerful dictator is largely a Nazi propaganda myth. Hitler's foreign policy had no overall design, and was really a spontaneous response to internal divisions.[10] Martin Broszat also sees very little

The role of Neville Chamberlain and appeasement

The orthodox view

Existing alongside the debate over Hitler's aims is an equally vast interest in the role of Neville Chamberlain and the policy of appeasement. The orthodox view of appeasement was put forward in *The guilty men*, published in 1940 by a number of British left-wing writers, under the pseudonym Cato. This defined appeasement as being the deliberate surrender of small nations in the face of Hitler's quite blatant bullying, and portrayed Chamberlain as 'the guiltiest of the guilty men' because he appeased Hitler from a position of weakness, at a time when all logic suggested that such a course of action was doomed to failure.[27] One of the first post-war studies of appeasement, by John Wheeler-Bennett, described the Munich Agreement of 1938 as a case study in the disease of political myopia which afflicted the leaders and peoples of Europe in the years between the wars. In Wheeler-Bennett's view, appeasement failed to appreciate that war is often preferable to peace at any price.[28] Many subsequent historians have produced equally critical accounts of appeasement. In Keith Middlemass' view, Chamberlain's policy of appeasement was a 'diplomacy of illusion', which was based on a defence strategy which did not protect Britain from an air attack, and on the fatal illusion that Hitler's aims were limited to a revision of the Treaty of Versailles. For these reasons, Chamberlain should be judged harshly, for he ran Britain's foreign policy as a one-man band, ignored the cabinet, deluded the public, and brushed aside all opposition.[29] The 'diplomacy of illusion' theory of appeasement is a modified version of the 'guilty men' thesis, and substitutes moral condemnation with deluded thinking, ineffective leadership and diplomatic bungling.

In more recent times, R. A. C. Parker has produced yet another critical interpretation of Chamberlain. He suggests that Chamberlain believed in appeasement as passionately as any religious zealot, and pursued it so single-mindedly that many possible alternatives, including a clear commitment to France, closer association with the League of Nations, and an alliance with the Soviet Union were completely rejected. The implication is that if Chamberlain had not been so stubborn in his belief in the benefits of appeasing Germany, then a barrier to Hitler's expansionism could have been built up earlier. According to this view, Chamberlain's conduct of British foreign policy ensured that, when war broke out, Britain and France had no major allies, and were also in a very weak military position.[30]

The revisionist view

Parker's interpretation goes against the current trend of treating Chamberlain and appeasement far more sympathetically. The turning point towards this widespread revisionism came in 1967, when the archives were opened up on the subject. Most revisionists avoid passing moral judgements on Chamberlain, and have broadened the analysis to include the discussion of social, economic and strategic factors.[31] The main essentials of the revisionist position are as follows.

1 A concentration on Chamberlain and the leading figures of the 'National Government' obscures the importance of a complex set of domestic, international, military and economic factors, which made a policy of standing up to the dictators impractical, and a policy of finding peace preferable.
2 British foreign policy during the 1930s should be viewed within an international context, which gives due emphasis to rival ideologies, economic systems and social groupings in Europe.
3 The leaders who took the decisions were prisoners of circumstances beyond their control.
4 British guilt for helping bring about the outbreak of war cannot be pinned exclusively on Chamberlain, who was an able and realistic politician who realised that Britain and France could not keep order in Europe, and who wanted Britain to retain its world-power status, which he believed would be lost in a second major world war.

In addition, the revisionists put forward three other important reasons why Chamberlain followed the policy of appeasement.

1 The British economy did not contain enough skilled workers to effect a large-scale rearmament programme without endangering the fragile British recovery from the great economic slump of the 1930s.
2 The military and naval chiefs constantly warned that Britain was not prepared for a simultaneous war against Germany, Italy and Japan, and advised the government to follow a policy of appeasement.
3 Public opinion consistently opposed rapid rearmament and a strong stand being taken against the dictators.

David Dilks, a leading revisionist, suggests that appeasement 'hoped for the best but prepared for the worst'; the key points of his recent re-evaluation of Chamberlain are as follows.

1 Appeasement grew out of the failure of the Paris Peace Settlement to create an effective balance of armed force in Europe, and to prevent a resurgence of German military force.
2 Chamberlain understood that the possession of military strength was crucial for a successful foreign policy, and based appeasement on the principle that Britain did not possess enough military force to prevent or deter Germany from achieving a revision of the Treaty of Versailles.
3 Chamberlain hoped that high-level negotiations might induce Hitler to resolve his grievances without resorting to force. However, this approach was accompanied by a preparation for the worst, achieved by constant increases in defence spending.

According to Dilks, Chamberlain was no deluded politician, but a complex character with a sharp mind, who wrestled with doubts over whether Hitler's aims were vast or limited. He wanted peace, because he genuinely hated the idea of war, but not peace at any price. Once Hitler showed that he was hell-bent on achieving European domination by force – which only seemed certain after the occupation of Czechoslovakia – then Chamberlain, with a heavy heart, decided to meet force with force.

As a result of the strength of the revisionists' arguments, supporters of the orthodox interpretation are now in the minority. Appeasement is no longer viewed as being a shameful policy based on surrender, but as a logical and realistic policy which gave Hitler every opportunity to solve German grievances short of war. However, perhaps the revisionists have had matters all their own way. This has led to the elevation of the status of Chamberlain by some ultra-revisionists to something of a national saviour, who might have saved the empire and have prevented a post-war British decline if only he had not lost his nerve and had allowed appeasement to continue.[32] Perhaps R. A. C. Parker, with his matchless knowledge of the documents on British foreign policy during the 1930s, has put a spoke in the wheel of the ultra-revisionists by showing the dangers of following a foreign policy with such single-minded certainty as Chamberlain showed in following appeasement. For Chamberlain, by the very strength of his political skill and tactical ability, convinced everyone, at a crucial time, that appeasement was the only logical course of action, and thereby demolished support for many alternative courses of action.

French foreign policy and the coming of war

The dominant positions occupied by Hitler's aims and Chamberlain's policy of appeasement have resulted in less attention being devoted to French foreign policy. A great many studies link British and French policy during the late 1930s.[33] The dominant view of inter-war France, which has not been greatly revised by subsequent research, is of a deeply divided and politically unstable country, which stumbled from crisis to crisis, from government to government, and from peace to war.[34] In such a politically divided society, the fall of France in 1940 was a certain eventuality. This orthodox view suggests that French foreign policy during the 1930s was obsessed with security and defence, had no intention of stopping Hitler by force, and willingly allowed Chamberlain to march France along the road to Munich. The reason why the French allowed Britain to take the lead was due to a fear of losing British support in a future war against Germany. In this respect, Anthony Adamthwaite argues that the architects of French foreign policy considered Anglo-French differences during the 1920s as something to be avoided in the face of the Nazi threat, and regarded Anglo-French agreement over their policy towards the dictators as being the best guarantee of French security.[35]

According to J-B. Duroselle, political decay and instability lay at the heart of the uncertainty, muddle and indecisiveness of French foreign policy.[36] There were no less than 16 different coalition governments in power between 1932 and 1940. René Girault regards 'impotence' as the key aspect of French policy, which, he suggests, was preparing, not for war, but for inevitable defeat.[37] The idea of France as being divided and rudderless, and heading for defeat, is emphasised in many studies. The French leaders of the 1930s are branded 'guilty men' whose reputations have not yet been fully rehabilitated. However, the British and French versions of appeasement sprang from differing motivations.[38] Chamberlain saw appeasement as a bold and positive policy, born of military weakness, but sympathetic to German grievances, while the French saw appeasement as a negative and stoical policy, illustrating that all their own efforts to prevent a German revival had failed. It appears that the French version of appeasement was a grim realisation of their past failures, with little deep sympathy for German grievances. Indeed, the solution of every German grievance during the 1930s led to a deepening French gloom. It seems that the French version of appeasement always feared the worst, and constantly worried about defeat.[39]

In Robert Young's view, French official thinking found the prospect of another war unthinkable, and therefore based its strategy on defence and diplomacy. The unwillingness of Britain to pledge full military support to France was a further factor which encouraged French policy meekly to follow the British lead.[40] Adamthwaite suggests that more energetic efforts by France might have won an alliance with Britain, but Ruth Henig is doubtful that such an alliance, or firmer action by France or Britain from 1936 to 1939, would have prevented war anyway. It might have brought war earlier, with probably the same outcome for France.[41]

An issue highlighted by many historians is the lack of boldness in French planning and tactics. As Robert Young shows, French military planning was based on the defence of the Maginot Line (a line of fortifications on France's eastern frontier), with no offensive plan. The leading French generals thought that Britain and France could hold Germany in western Europe and win a long-drawn-out war, but they feared a Franco-German war with Britain remaining on the sidelines,[42] and urged French leaders to ensure that they did not lose British support. This can be seen as a very sensible decision. By allowing Chamberlain to take the lead, the French government drew Britain into the issue of the security of eastern Europe. Even the failure of the Munich settlement, which was such a disaster for Chamberlain, was actually helpful to France: it drew Britain into closer alliance with France, and further committed it to the defence of eastern Europe. This is what French leaders had wanted all along. Perhaps historians, mindful of the French collapse in 1940, have judged French policy too harshly, and Chamberlain's appeasement too sympathetically.

Mussolini's role in the origins of the Second World War

The orthodox view

The role of Mussolini's Italy in the events which led to the Second World War has also aroused significant historical interest. Mussolini was the first European fascist dictator: he undermined the Paris Peace Settlement, aided Franco during the Spanish Civil War, played a crucial role at the Munich

Conference, signed the Pact of Steel, remained neutral in September 1939, and finally joined the war on Hitler's side in 1940. Few historians would deny that Mussolini was a disruptive force in international relations during the 1930s.[43] The orthodox view of Mussolini's foreign policy suggests that it was ineffective, immoral, designed to grab headlines and to please Italian public opinion, and lacked any clear objectives. Gaetano Salvemini portrayed Mussolini as an 'irresponsible improviser', who was gifted only in the art of propaganda, and conducted foreign policy with a view to gaining short-term popularity for his precarious fascist regime.[44] Elizabeth Wiskemann claimed that Mussolini rolled his eyes, brandished his chin and shouted cruel phrases, but had no idea what his goals in foreign policy were.[45] Denis Mack Smith called Mussolini an opportunist who 'lived in cloud-cuckoo land and improvised his foreign policy almost daily'.[46] A. J. P. Taylor saw Mussolini as a vain, blundering boaster, with an ill-informed, uncertain and vacillating foreign policy which was 'as unpredictable as the weather'.[47] These unflattering views of Mussolini quickly became the established interpretation.

The revisionist view

However, a host of revisionist historians have successfully challenged this view. MacGregor Knox suggests that the depiction of Mussolini as an opportunist cannot prove that he did not have a coherent set of aims in his foreign policy. The most important were to achieve *spazio vitale* ('living space') for Italians in North Africa and the Middle East, and to transform Italy into a major imperial power to rank alongside Britain and France. The overwhelming German victory over France in 1940 allowed Mussolini to pursue these long-standing aims.[48] For many historians, there was a 'primacy of domestic politics' in Mussolini's conduct of foreign policy. For George Baer, the most consistent element was Mussolini's desire to use foreign-policy adventures as a 'safety valve' with which to divert public attention from domestic pressures.[49] In Renzo de Felice's view, Mussolini's policy made for mischief but 'excluded the possibility of a European war' and looked for cheap imperial gains with which to boost Mussolini's popularity.[50] However, many historians have suggested that Mussolini's foreign policy was deeply influenced by the external limitations of the Italian power-political position in European affairs. In Cassel's opinion, Italy was a major power by courtesy title only, and did not possess the economic or military resources to take a decisive lead. Therefore, Italy, as the weakest of the major European powers, had to pursue a policy of 'equilibrium' among the major powers.[51]

Mussolini and Germany

The most frequently discussed aspect of Mussolini's foreign policy is the question of his relations with Nazi Germany. In D. C. Watt's view, the Rome–Berlin Axis was really an exercise in myth-making, and implied no fundamentally close ideological affinity between the two dictators.[52] Mack Smith believes that Mussolini signed the Pact of Steel with Hitler in 1939 in order to frighten Britain and France into offering further imperial gains to Italy. This type of interpretation leans heavily towards the idea of Mussolini always keeping his options open. Yet some historians are willing to take Mussolini's pro-German stance more seriously. In this respect, Philip Morgan has recently suggested that the Pact of Steel between Hitler and Mussolini represented the expression of parallel desires in the minds of the two dictators to achieve their aims by alliance in war. For Morgan, the strategic weakness of Italy forced Mussolini to stay on the sidelines, but once Germany had defeated France Mussolini could follow what his real heart desired.[53] However, it is possible to suggest that Italian power-political self-interest, not fascist ideology, lay at the heart of both decisions. By opting for neutrality in 1939, when the outcome of the war was uncertain, Mussolini was seeking to keep his options open, and by joining Hitler in 1940, when it seemed that Germany would win the war, Mussolini was seeking to gain the best advantage for Italy. Even so, it is very difficult to decide whether Mussolini's actions are evidence of growing parallel ideological designs by the two fascist powers, which is plausible, or whether Mussolini's foreign policy was always designed to gain the best advantage for Italy, which is probably more convincing.

The Soviet Union and the origins of the Second World War

The 'collective-security approach'

The role of the Nazi–Soviet Non-aggression Pact of August 1939, which made war in Europe inevitable, as well as the motives of Soviet foreign policy during the 1930s, have also been key issues within the historical debate.[54] The Nazi–Soviet Pact has been viewed as 'Stalin's blank cheque to Hitler', which virtually guaranteed war, and as 'the pinnacle of Stalin's diplomacy'. During the era of the Cold War, the debate suffered from the bias displayed by many Soviet and American historians. According to Soviet historians, writing before the collapse of the former communist regime, Stalin's foreign policy attempted to uphold the principles of collective security against Hitler, and reluctantly moved towards signing the Nazi–Soviet Pact because Britain and France deliberately appeased Hitler, undermined the League of Nations, and delayed signing a triple alliance in 1939 to deter Nazi Germany.[55]

This sympathetic interpretation of Soviet foreign policy is dubbed the 'collective-security approach',[56] and has found widespread support from historians outside the former Soviet Union. A. J. P. Taylor acknowledged that opportunism and tactical flexibility were key aspects of Stalin's diplomacy, but he still suggested that Soviet foreign policy during the 1930s was defensive and supported the use of collective security as the best means of stopping Hitler. In Taylor's view, it was the delaying tactics of Chamberlain in 1939 which forced Stalin to sign the Nazi–Soviet Pact. However, Jonathan Haslam suggests that Soviet foreign policy during the 1930s was neither principled nor unprincipled, but was based on pure national self-interest, and looked for a course of action which would provide the greatest degree of security.[57]

The 'collective-security approach' regarding Soviet foreign policy is given further support by Geoffrey Roberts, who views Soviet foreign policy as being a mixture of ideology, expediency, Utopian and realistic calculations, innovation and classical diplomacy. The central objective was peaceful co-existence with all the major capitalist states. According to Roberts, Stalin's assessment of the delicate international situation led to a genuine desire to uphold collective security, a desire which found no support from Britain and France during the late 1930s. After the Munich Agreement in 1938, Stalin viewed the League of Nations as a spent force, and became deeply mistrustful of the aims of the appeasers, whom, he felt, were happy as long as Hitler moved east. Thus, Roberts suggests that the development of events prompted the Soviet Union to opt for an isolationist policy designed to avoid a war with Nazi Germany. According to this view, the Nazi–Soviet Pact was an isolationist form of protection from war with Nazi Germany.[58]

The view of American historians during the Cold War

However, the 'collective-security approach' is often viewed as being much too sympathetic towards Soviet foreign policy. During the Cold War era, many American historians portrayed Stalin's foreign policy in a very different way. It was William Langer and S. Everett Gleason who defined the Nazi–Soviet Pact as 'Stalin's blank cheque' to Hitler, which virtually guaranteed that war would start in 1939.[59] Robert Tucker went further, and suggested that Soviet foreign policy during the 1930s wanted to divide the capitalist states against each other to ensure that they plunged into war, exhausted each other on the field of battle, and left the Soviet Union well placed to make substantial territorial gains in eastern Europe.[60] All these historians felt that Stalin's support for collective security was a cynical ploy to mask an underlying desire for a Nazi–Soviet pact. However, a great many of such interpretations were deeply coloured by the prevailing hostile climate between east and west during the era of the Cold War.

The view of the 'German school'

More recently, a 'German school' of historians, which draws primarily on German archives, has assigned significant responsibility to Stalin for the outbreak of war. These German historians have suggested that Soviet foreign policy during the 1930s desired a reconstruction of the close Soviet–German relationship, established by the co-operative Soviet–German Treaty of Rapallo in 1922, and broken off by Hitler in 1933. They believe that Stalin wanted to renew the Rapallo relationship, and was finally given the chance by Hitler in 1939. Such interpretations regard the Soviet Union as giving Hitler the 'green light' for aggression in 1939, and therefore apportion significant responsibility for the start of the war to the Soviet Union.[61] The most extreme version of the 'German school' was put forward by Ernst Topitsch, who views the Second World War as 'Stalin's war', and makes the following points in support of this interpretation.

1 The view of Hitler as being the leading character in the events which led to the Second World War has been exaggerated and requires modification.
2 Stalin was the key figure in the outbreak of war and the key victor of the war.
3 Stalin was the only leader in Europe with clear aims.
4 Stalin set out to start a European war in 1939 between what he saw as aggressive and non-aggressive capitalist states, which left the Soviet Union in a neutral position and well placed to reap a rich reward.

According to this view, the Second World War was a Soviet attack on the Western capitalist democracies, with Hitler acting as Stalin's unwitting agent.[62]

However, P. M. H. Bell suggests that this theory, which is based on no new documentary evidence, is pure conjecture. Specifically, the idea of Stalin having a clear plan for the Soviet domination of Europe remains conjecture.[63] The Soviet Union's incredible lack of preparation for the German attack in June 1941 must raise doubts about whether such a plan ever existed. On the whole, most German interpretations wish to assign part of the blame for the war on Stalin as a co-conspirator with Hitler, and equally to suggest that Stalin had vast aims for European domination. This is a case of confusing the outcome of the war, which produced a Soviet victory at enormous cost, with its causes. To accept the views of the 'German school', we have to believe that the Soviet Union followed a foreign policy which it never believed in. The recent opening of Soviet archives by the new democratic governments of the Russian Federation has revealed that the Soviet entry into the League of Nations; its offer to save Czechoslovakia in 1938; the speeches by Litvinov, the Soviet foreign minister, at the League of Nations in support of collective security; the denouncements of fascism and appeasement by Stalin; and the preference, in 1939, for an agreement with Britain and France, do all appear to have been genuine. It is difficult to accept that Hitler's role in the origins of the Second World should be placed below the actions of Stalin.

'The primacy of internal politics'

Another important approach to the Soviet role in the origins of the Second World War focuses on the 'the primacy of internal politics',[64] and concentrates on internal influences on the formation of Soviet foreign policy. It points to key divisions within Stalin's regime over the direction of foreign policy: on the one hand, a significant group favoured a return to a close Soviet–German friendship; on the other, a larger group supported collective security. The course of events allowed the pro-German group to shift opinion away from collective security towards the Nazi–Soviet Pact. However, the extent, depth and character of the internal Soviet differences can be exaggerated. The major Soviet desire was to search for a foreign policy which would prevent it being involved in war. It is difficult to believe that Stalin allowed wide-ranging differences to exist in the field of foreign policy, but insisted on brutal conformity to his decisions on domestic policy. The majority of historians would suggest that Stalin was inward looking and determined to 'build socialism in one country', and therefore desired a defensive foreign policy.

The role of external events was probably more influential than that of any internal disagreements. The Munich Agreement left a very deep impression on Stalin, as he saw it as the death knell of any hope for a collective front against Hitler involving Britain and France. Thus, in Hildebrand's view, 'the foundations of the Nazi–Soviet Pact were laid at Munich'.[65]

The Paris Peace Settlement and its consequences

The orthodox view

Discussion of the fragility of the 1919 Paris Peace Settlement is another key feature of the historical debate. A great many historians have viewed the settlement as being a failed compromise between the idealism of Wilson, the US president, and the realism and selfishness of the European powers. The very titles of books on the Paris Peace Settlement – *The economic consequences of the peace*, *The lost peace* and *The twenty-year crisis* – reflect the usually negative verdict of historians. As James Joll puts it, 'Europe was divided by the peace conference into those who wanted the peace revised [Germany, Italy, Japan and Hungary] and those who wanted it upheld [France, Poland, Czechoslovakia, Yugoslavia]', and those who were not that interested [the USA and Britain].[66]

For E. H. Carr, the Paris Peace Settlement was based on unworkable idealistic principles, most notably national self-determination and collective security, but the fundamental weakness of the settlement was its failure to solve the 'German problem'. This view was supported by A. J. P. Taylor, who suggested that the Treaty of Versailles was crushing, vindictive, and lacked moral validity, because no German accepted it as a fair settlement and all Germans wanted to shake it off. For Taylor, the Second World War was really 'a war over the settlement of Versailles; a war which had been implicit when the First World War ended because the peacemakers had not solved the German problem'.[67] The failure of the Paris Peace Settlement to create a viable balance of power in Europe has been seen as a vital weakness. In P. M. H. Bell's opinion, the settlement was 'a rickety edifice which was unstable from the start'.[68] At the heart of its weak foundations was, in Anthony Lentin's view, a failure to tackle the underlying potential of Germany. The peacemakers did not seem to realise that the collapse of the Russian, Habsburg and Ottoman empires left Germany in a potentially stronger position in Europe than ever before. The newly constituted nation states of central and eastern Europe were small, weak, ethnically divided, and open to domination by a resurgent Germany.[69]

The revisionist view

However, many historians also offer a much more sympathetic interpretation of the Paris Peace Settlement. Adamthwaite views it as a brave attempt to deal with intractable, perhaps insoluble, problems. For Ruth Henig, the settlement was 'a creditable achievement' which failed because of the severe economic and social problems left by the war; major divisions among the peacemakers about the terms of the settlement; and, most importantly, the reluctance of political leaders during the inter-war period to enforce it. According to this view, the architects of the Paris Peace Settlement failed to follow through the principles laid down at Paris and by their failure ensured a German revival, and with further doses of indecisiveness brought about war.[70]

Paul Birdsall considers the refusal of the USA to become involved in upholding the Paris Peace Settlement as a crucial reason for the settlement's subsequent failure. This destroyed the prospects of building a successful League of Nations and the forging of a democratic front with which to uphold the settlement. Paul Kennedy points out the great differences between the success of the settlement during the 1920s, when it worked, and during the 1930s, when it was crushed by the combined militarism of Germany, Japan and Italy. For Kennedy, the crucial reason for its collapse was the Great Depression of the early 1930s, which destroyed international co-operation and encouraged extreme selfishness to dominate international relations. The Depression also helped to destroy German democracy and contributed to Hitler's rise to power, and it was his dictatorship which brought war.

Economic interpretations

The Marxist view

The role of economic factors in causing the outbreak of the Second World War is an important, if neglected, part of the debate. In Richard Overy's view, 'No single factor was more important in explaining the breakdown of the diplomatic system in the 1930s than the world economic crisis'.[71] Many Marxist historians go further, and claim that the Second World War was due to an unresolved economic crisis in the capitalist system.[72] At the heart of this crisis was the drift towards fascism in Germany. Economic depression increased the desire of German monopoly capitalists to seek the lifeboat of Nazism to shield them from the unpredictable waters of modern capitalism. This interpretation views Hitler as being a convenient front man for those monopoly capitalists who wished to destroy organised labour and shield German industry from foreign competition. However, studies of 'big business' and the rise of Hitler have shown that Nazism was seen as a last, not a first, resort for German capitalists.[73] Tim Mason has demonstrated a clear 'primacy of politics' over the needs of industrial capitalists in the decision-making process of the Third Reich. Most non-Marxist historians (which is what most historians are) reject the view of Nazism being reared and controlled by capitalist interests.[74]

The role of capitalist interests

However, to deny completely a close relationship between Nazism and capitalist interests in Germany is considered by Ian Kershaw to be far too complacent. Many powerful German industrialists favoured the breakdown of Weimar democracy, and saw the weakening of organised labour through an authoritarian regime as being an essential prerequisite for a restoration of profits. The Nazi Party may have been a last resort for 'big business', but once in power it provided a type of rule which benefited the financial position of industrial capitalists greatly. This is not to say that Hitler was a mere puppet of capitalist interests, but his regime was quite clearly not directed against their interests. In any cost–benefit analysis of the groups which gained the most from Nazi rule, industrial monopoly capitalists come very near the top. Many industrial companies, particularly those linked to rearmament, showed a quite remarkable increase in profits during the Nazi era.

On the other hand, Hildebrand claims that the Nazi economy was in the 'service of politics', not monopoly capitalists, and suggests that Hitler virtually 'eliminated' industrialists as a major political factor in Nazi Germany.[75] There is little evidence of industrialists having had a direct influence on foreign policy. William Carr suggests that ideological, strategic and economic factors were too closely intermeshed in German foreign policy to permit their clinical separation. Within this complex relationship, the mutual dependence of the Nazi leadership and industry was clearly a significant factor.[76] Ian Kershaw views the alliance between the Nazi leadership and the industrial–military complex, which was cemented by rearmament and the expansionist programme, as being central to the survival of the regime, right up until the end of the Third Reich.[77]

The German economic crisis

This raises the issue of the German economic situation, and its relation to Hitler's decision to go to war in 1939. Tim Mason suggests that the German decision for war is related to vast rearmament and to the failure of Hitler's economic policy to deliver a high level of consumer spending. Mason suggests that in 1939 the German economy was in crisis, a crisis only capable of resolution by either cutting defence expenditure, which Hitler thought unthinkable, or by embarking on a war of economic plunder in order to avoid economic collapse. In support, David Kaiser has shown how each Nazi occupation was designed to secure additional economic resources. According to this view, the economic policy of Hitler actually created a crisis which pushed him into what he hoped would be limited wars against small powers.

However, the idea of an economic crisis being the primary reason for the German decision for war has been challenged. Richard Overy has shown that the economic problems facing the Germany economy during the late 1930s were not so great as to require wars of mere plunder with which to resolve them. In Overy's view, power-politics dominated economic considerations in Hitler's foreign policy. The decision for war in 1939 was part of his plan to dominate Europe, even though he hoped that the war with Poland might be localised. Put this way, the Second World War was viewed by Hitler as 'a power-political struggle' fought for the old-fashioned imperial ideal of territorial gain. It remains doubtful whether economic factors dominated power-political factors when Hitler made major decisions on foreign policy.[78]

The role of ideology

Perhaps ideology was a more important driving force in the outbreak of the Second World War. It is tempting to view the Second World War not as a struggle of great powers pursuing traditional national interests, but as a conflict of competing ideologies. The inter-war period saw the emergence of three mutually exclusive ideological groupings.

1 Germany, Italy and Japan had regimes which expressed ideologies favourable to fervent nationalism and military aggression.
2 The Soviet Union, established by the 1917 revolution, was led by supporters of Marxist-Leninist ideas who initially preached a doctrine of 'world-wide revolution'.
3 Britain, France and the USA were democratic nations with free elections, capitalist economies, and foreign policies which favoured peace.

These deep ideological differences made international harmony very difficult to achieve; each major power was often pulling in a different direction. Thus, if a key cause of all wars is a breakdown of diplomatic harmony, then ideology must have made a significant contribution to the origins of the Second World War.

Totalitarianism

For Hannah Arendt, the emergence of totalitarian states, which were fundamentally anti-capitalist and anti-democratic with a natural inclination towards 'military conquest', was the key cause of the Second World War. She views all totalitarian regimes, whether of the left or of the right, as exhibiting similar political characteristics: they were all led by a 'mob mentality' geared to political terror at home and armed aggression abroad.[79] This theory postulates six central components of a totalitarian state:

1 an official ideology directed towards a historical goal which is instilled into the entire population;
2 a single, mass party, led by a single, dominant individual;
3 a brutal secret police;
4 monopoly control over the mass media;
5 a monopoly over weapons; and
6 coercion and central control of the entire economy.

Other historians suggest that a 'revolutionary dynamic' is central to all totalitarian regimes, which are 'closed regimes' that allow no freedom for the individual.

The concept of totalitarianism was used as far back as 1923 to describe Mussolini's rule in Italy. During the 1930s, comparisons were made between the Soviet Union and Hitler's Germany. The term was made popular after 1945, and was most often used in Cold War propaganda struggles to emphasise the benefits of free democratic rule over totalitarian rule. The implication was clear: all totalitarian regimes were pretty much the same. Hitler and Stalin were both brutal dictators, both were 'sinful', both threatened world peace, both aimed at world domination, and both should never have been appeased. Few historians would deny that Stalin's domination of the Soviet Union was a very brutal form of personal rule which fits the totalitarian concept quite well. However, the idea that all totalitarian regimes favour military aggression does not fit Soviet foreign policy during the 1930s. As discussed above, most of Stalin's actions in foreign affairs in the years leading to war were primarily defensive.

Fascism and the road to war

This does not mean that the role of ideology in the origins of war has been totally rejected. The real problem may have been fascism. The troublemakers in foreign policy during the 1930s were Germany, Italy and Japan, which all had fascist (or nationalist) regimes which weakened democracy and socialism, increased arms expenditure, and engaged in foreign-policy adventures. However, trying to fit the regimes of Germany, Japan and Italy into a single concept of fascism has proved very disappointing.[80] Italian fascism was less brutal, totalitarian and ideologically driven than German National Socialism, and even though Mussolini did glorify the use of armed force, his foreign policy was driven as much by strategic and diplomatic calculations of national self-interest as by ideology. The idea of 'Japanese fascism' was popularised by Barrington Moore, who saw Japan and Germany as 'industrial-feudal' societies demonstrating 'repression at home and aggression abroad'.[81] However, there was no single leader in Japan, no single, mass party, and no mass terror. Japan may have been 'militarist' and 'highly authoritarian', but Japanese foreign policy grew out of internal divisions and strategic weakness, and showed very little sign of an ideological pattern.

This leaves us back where we started, with Hitler and National Socialism in Germany. The powerful economic and strategic position of Nazi Germany gave it more opportunity of putting its ideology into action. Nazism was projected as being the will of a single, powerful individual – Adolf Hitler – in control of a single party, and put great emphasis on strong armed forces and a dynamic and challenging foreign policy. The drums, the jackboots, the flags, the military parades, and the salutes to the all-powerful *Führer*, can all be seen as part of the definite creation of a momentum for war. It is difficult to deny that militarism, marching and war were all essential aspects of Nazism. However, militarism was not an ideological invention of Nazism, nor was the German desire to dominate Europe. It is possible to suggest that Hitler followed a classic tradition of all great powers with a military advantage and a desire for expansionism. He often linked his own aims with those of Frederick the Great (the eighteenth-century 'soldier-king' of Prussia) – not with those of the Kaiser. However, the policy of *Lebensraum* does seem to have contained a clear, and perhaps unique, ideological dimension, in so far as Hitler wished systematically to exterminate Jewish and Slavic people, and to expand the German population into the vacant 'living space'. Even so, Hitler's foreign policy from 1933 to 1939, the years which led to war, was not always driven by ideological aims. On many occasions Hitler was willing to compromise his ideology in order to suit a specific diplomatic situation.

The debate over the origins of the Asian-Pacific conflict

The debate over the origins of the Asian-Pacific war is a distinctly separate area of research. The Japanese attack on Pearl Harbour seems to present the historian with little difficulty in deciding which power was most responsible for the outbreak of war. The Tokyo war tribunal, held at the end of the Second World War, portrayed Japanese leaders as the cold-blooded planners of the Asian-Pacific war, with the USA the injured party and a reluctant belligerent.[82] This view soon achieved the level of mythical status, and was accepted even by Japanese historians. For example, Muruyama suggested that imperial Japan steamed like a locomotive from a bourgeois revolution in the nineteenth century towards a fascism that cold-bloodedly planned the Asian-Pacific war. However, the idea of a premeditated plan on the part of the Japanese government to start the Asian-Pacific war has been challenged by a wide range of revisionist historians, who regard the USA as no innocent bystander in the events which led to war. At the centre of the debate over the outbreak of the Asian-Pacific war are the roles of Japanese and US foreign policy.

Japan and the origins of the Asian-Pacific conflict

Japan was at war for a much longer period than any of the other combatants of the Second World War. There has been great debate about why Japan embarked on such a disastrous series of complex wars with China, the USA and the British Empire, which ultimately ended in defeat.[83] The most detailed Japanese study of foreign policy on the subject is entitled *The road to the Pacific war*, which draws on over 5,000 documents and provides the most sophisticated and detailed interpretation of why Japan went to war. The main findings of this vast study are as follows.

1 The Japanese government was reluctantly dragged into war with China in 1937 because it felt that Japanese interests in China were being threatened by the growth of Chinese nationalism.
2 Japan had no co-ordinated foreign, military or naval policy during the 1930s, and no detailed programme of aggression in the Asian-Pacific region.
3 The war with China became costly and protracted, and forced the Japanese government to consider gaining territory elsewhere in Southeast Asia.
4 The defeat of France in 1940 led Japanese leaders seriously to plan to gain territory in Southeast Asia.
5 Japanese leaders thought that they could advance in Southeast Asia without provoking a war with the USA.
6 The US decision in July 1941 to impose a financial and oil embargo on Japan produced a fatalism within the Japanese government, which now saw the USA as being a key barrier to Japanese designs in Southeast Asia.

According to this view, a cumulative and complex series of factors – most notably the stalemate in the war with China, the US oil embargo, and the opportunities which the advance of Germany in Europe opened up for the seizure of Dutch, French and British colonies in Southeast Asia – encouraged Japan. It was the opportunities opened up during the Second World War which helped to push Japan towards a bold expansionist drive into Southeast Asia and the gamble to attack the US fleet at Pearl Harbour. This interpretation suggests that the pressure of events, and the opportunities that they presented, inexorably led Japan towards war in the Asian-Pacific region. In this view, the crisis of Pearl Harbour arose because the USA had decided to place pressure on Japan to cease any further expansion in the Asian-Pacific region, and because Japan refused to bow to American pressure.[84] This Japanese study has influenced many subsequent Western studies of the Japanese role in the origins of the Asian-Pacific war.

In a very important study on the origins of the Second World War in Asia and the Pacific, Akira Iriye shows that the underlying desire of Japanese foreign policy to gain a dominant position in Asia and the Pacific increasingly came into conflict with the growing US desire to prevent Japanese expansion in the region. In Iriye's view, US–Japanese relations had seriously deteriorated during the 1930s, and even before the imposition of the oil and trade embargo in 1941 the general trend of US policy had been anti-Japanese. Even so, Iriye suggests that the Japanese decision for war grew out of the short-term crisis in US–Japanese relations in 1941. He shows that the actual Japanese decision to launch a simultaneous assault on Pearl Harbour and British, Dutch and US possessions in Southeast Asia was only firmly decided upon in November 1941. In Iriye's view, the Japanese government saw the attack on Pearl Harbour as the beginning of a struggle for a new order in Southeast Asia.[85]

However, the extent to which Japanese policy-makers were obsessed with the USA can be exaggerated. According to Hosoya, it was China which dominated Japanese foreign-policy objectives during the 1930s – not hostility towards the USA – and he suggests that Japanese expansion in Southeast Asia during 1941 grew as an unplanned consequence of Japan becoming bogged down in its war with China (in which it had been involved since 1937) and its need for fresh supplies of oil and raw materials.[86] The actual events of the European war also had an impact: the fall of France and Holland in June 1940 opened the door to the possibility of major territorial gains for Japan in Southeast Asia. The US oil and trade embargo threatened this advance, and led Japan to make a bold strike at Pearl Harbour. In Hosoya's opinion, Japan's aggressive policy in Southeast Asia grew after the German advance in Europe, and can be viewed as being unplanned and opportunistic. It seems that the army hoped that Japanese domination in Southeast Asia could be achieved without a war with the USA, while the navy – the key planner of the attack on Pearl Harbour, and the prime advocate of a forward drive in Southeast Asia – did not have a key influence on Japanese foreign policy until 1940. The primary concern of the Japanese army was to win the war with China, and it only seems to have given its support to the navy's idea of an attack on Pearl Harbour, followed by an assault on Southeast Asia, when the US imposed the oil embargo.[87]

All this research has served to show that Japan's attack on Pearl Harbour did not come out of the blue, but was part of a complex series of events. There was no inevitable Japanese road to war with the USA. The attack on Pearl Harbour was an opportunistic gamble which grew out of the serious impasse in relations between Japan and the USA in 1941. It was caused as much by the US decision to introduce an oil and trade embargo as by Japanese design. The Japanese road to war was very complex: the Japanese government, the army and the navy all pursued different, often contradictory policies, which makes the idea of an unfolding Japanese programme of aggression designed to bring a major Asian-Pacific war so difficult to sustain.

The role of the USA in the origins of the Asian-Pacific war

This more complex picture of Japan's road to war has meant that the USA is no longer seen as being a completely innocent bystander in the origins of the Asian-Pacific conflict. The traditional view of American foreign policy during the years which led to war focuses on the isolationism and neutrality which formed such a key part of US foreign policy under Franklin D. Roosevelt. According to Robert Devine, American foreign policy under Roosevelt was 'sterile and bankrupt' in the face of a mounting international crisis, and was actually saved from total disrepute by the Japanese decision to attack Pearl Harbour, which finally forced the USA to take a stand against military aggression.[88]

However, the policies of Roosevelt towards Japan have been viewed as a significant factor in the outbreak of the Asian-Pacific war. In Paul Schroeder's view, the Pacific war was 'unnecessary and avoidable', and was caused as much by 'Roosevelt's excessive moralism' against Japan, and his fervent desire to join the European war, as by any clear programme of Japanese aggression.[89] This interpretation emphasises how the growing success of Germany in the European war galvanised Roosevelt into an active desire to find some pretext with which to swing American public opinion around to the idea of the USA becoming a participant in the Second World War. Put this way, Roosevelt's decision to freeze Japanese assets in the USA and to impose an oil embargo in July 1941 was a deliberately provocative act which left Japan with two alternatives: to give in to American pressure, or to launch a strike in Southeast Asia to secure vital oil supplies. The most extreme version of this line of argument was put forward by Harry Elmer Barnes, who suggested that Roosevelt quite deliberately goaded the Japanese into war during 1941 and also exposed the US fleet at Pearl Harbour to a Japanese attack.

A great mystery still surrounds the question about why the US fleet was so incredibly unprepared for the Japanese strike at Pearl Harbour, but no convincing evidence has ever surfaced with which to implicate Roosevelt or the US government.[90] Nevertheless, it is agreed by most historians that Roosevelt knew full well that his belligerent stand towards Japan would be likely to produce a violent response. The mystery deepens further when we realise that the US government had successfully decoded Japanese telegrams by December 1941, and that it expected a Japanese attack on Siam (modern-day Thailand). Of course, many historians have speculated whether US officials in Washington decoded the Japanese plans to attack Pearl Harbour and deliberately kept these plans from the naval commander at Pearl Harbour. The evidence of Admiral Kimmel, the US naval commander at Pearl Harbour, indicates that US officials in Washington led him to believe that the Japanese had no plans to strike at Pearl Harbour. Perhaps Robert Ferrell is on the right track when he suggests that the leading figures in foreign and defence policy in the Roosevelt administration knew that the Japanese were likely to take some drastic action, but they seemed to rule out a surprise Japanese strike at Pearl Harbour.[91]

However, it is wrong to attribute all the blame to US policy for the outbreak of the Asian-Pacific conflict. It seems clear that the Japanese government had no desire to make concessions to the US government over its war with China, or to modify its plans to make territorial gains in Southeast Asia. On the other hand, American leaders in 1941 knew that a war between Japan and the USA was a distinct possibility after the oil and financial embargo had been imposed. In this respect, Iriye suggests that the USA, with the firm support of Britain, had decided to take a united stand against the growing Japanese threat in the Asian-Pacific region. Hence the crisis of 1941 was a test of strength between the USA and Britain on the one hand, and Japan on the other. The aim of this

In what ways does this American propaganda poster, produced soon after the Japanese attack on Pearl Harbour, reflect American attitudes to the Asian-Pacific conflict?

provocative stance was to induce Japanese leaders to abandon their expansionist designs on Southeast Asia. The belligerent stand of Roosevelt in 1941 was a clear abandonment of the American policy of isolationism, and was greatly influenced by British and US military officials, who advised the US president that Japan would be easily defeated in Southeast Asia, both on land and at sea. However, Japan was no mere imperial pawn of Britain or the USA in the Asian-Pacific region. By 1941, Japanese leaders felt that they had enough military strength with which to establish a dominant position in Southeast Asia, and were not prepared to be deflected from this aim by either Roosevelt – who had previously failed to match strong words of moral condemnation with military action – nor the British, who had not performed well in their battles with Nazi Germany.

A. J. P. Taylor's view

- War broke out not because of Hitler's plan, but because of Chamberlain's blunders.
- War was the logical conclusion of the course of German history from 1871 to 1945.

The orthodox view

- Hitler was following a master plan to gain *Lebensraum*, to destroy the Soviet Union, to gain territory in the Middle East, and ultimately to win global domination.
- Appeasement was a deliberate surrender to Hitler.
- The Nazi–Soviet Pact was Stalin's 'blank cheque' to Hitler.
- Totalitarian regimes inevitably inclined towards war.
- Japan cold-bloodedly planned war; the USA was the injured party.

Revisionist views

- Hitler's aggressive foreign policy was a response to internal German divisions.
- Hitler was an opportunist rather than being driven by his ideology.
- Appeasement sought peace.
- The flawed Paris Peace Settlement is ultimately to blame for the failure of appeasement.
- The Paris Peace Settlement failed because of the failure of the USA to uphold it.
- Stalin was forced into the Nazi–Soviet Pact by the failure of collective security.
- Stalin wanted a European war from which the Soviet Union would gain.
- The cost of the war with China forced Japan to seize territory in Southeast Asia.
- The war in Europe gave Japan the opportunity to seize European colonies.
- The US embargos forced Japan to attack the USA.
- Roosevelt provoked Japan into attacking Pearl Harbour as a pretext for entering the war.

Other views

- War was due to an unresolved crisis in Europe's capitalist systems.
- Hitler needed a war of economic plunder in order to avoid Germany's economic collapse.

Figure 2. The historians' debate over the origins of the Second World War.

Notes and references

1 J. Snell (ed.), *The outbreak of the Second World War*, London, 1962, p. vii.

2 A. J. P. Taylor, *The origins of the Second World War*, London, 1961.

3 For a detailed discussion of the Taylor controversy, see G. Martel (ed.), *The origins of the Second World War reconsidered: the A. J. P. Taylor debate after 25 years*, London, 1986.

4 For detailed discussion of the debate over Hitler's foreign policy, see K. Bracher, 'The role of Hitler: perspectives of interpretation', in W. Laqueur (ed.), *Fascism: a reader's guide*, London, 1979; J. Hiden and J. Farquharson, *Explaining Hitler's Germany*, London, 1983; K. Hildebrand, *The Third Reich*, London, 1984; and I. Kershaw, *The Nazi dictatorship: problems and perspectives of interpretation*, London, 3rd edn, 1993.

5 See H. R. Trevor-Roper, 'The mind of Adolf Hitler', the foreword to his *Hitler's table talk*, London, 1953.

6 A Bullock, *Hitler: a study in tyranny*, London, revised edn, 1964. See also A. Bullock, 'Hitler and the origins of the Second World War', in E. M. Robertson (ed.), *The origins of the Second World War*, London, 1971.

7 Kershaw, *Nazi dictatorship*, p. 110.

8 K. Hildebrand, *The foreign policy of the Third Reich*, London, 1973.

9 This school of historians has been dubbed 'intentionalists'.

10 K. D. Bracher, *The German dictatorship*, London, 1973.

11 M. Broszat, *The Hitler state*, London, 1981.

12 H. Mommsen, 'National Socialism: continuity and change', in Laqueur (ed.), *Fascism*.

13 See F. Meinecke, *The German catastrophe: reflections and recollections*, Boston, 1950.

14 R. J. B. Bosworth, *Explaining Auschwitz and Hiroshima, history-writing and the Second World War*, London, 1993, p. 62.

15 R. Dahrendorf, *Society and democracy in Germany*, London, 1966.

16 See Kershaw, *Nazi dictatorship*, pp. 131–49.

17 D. Puekert, *Inside Nazi Germany: conformity and opposition in everyday life*, London, 1987.

18 For a discussion of recent trends in research, see R. Geary, *Hitler and Nazism*, London, pp. 37–61.

19 See T. Childers, *The Nazi voter*, New Jersey, 1983.

20 The argument is put forward in L. B. Namier, *1848: the revolution of the intellectuals*, London, 1946.

21 A. J. P. Taylor, *The course of German history: a survey of the development of German history since 1815*, revised edn, London, 1961, p. vii.

22 See F. Fischer, *From Kaiserreich to Third Reich: elements of continuity in German history, 1871–1945*, London, 1986.

23 See G. Eley, 'Conservatives and radical nationalists in Germany: the production of fascist potentials, 1912–28', in M. Blinkhorn (ed.), *Fascists and conservatives*, London, 1994.

24 G. Craig, *Germany, 1866–1945*, Oxford, 1968.

25 For a discussion, see R. J. Evans, 'From Hitler to Bismarck: Third Reich and Kaiserreich in recent historiography, Part II', *Historical Journal*, vol. 26 (1984).

26 Eley, 'Conservatives and radical nationalists', in Blinkhorn (ed.), *Fascists and conservatives*.

27 Cato, *The guilty men*, London, 1940. The controversy surrounding the book is discussed in S. Astor, 'Guilty men: the case of Neville Chamberlain', in R. Boyce and E. M. Robertson (eds.), *Paths to war: new essays on the origins of the Second World War*, London, 1989. See also F. McDonough, 'Chamberlain: guilty man or national saviour?', *History Review*, no. 23 (1995).

28 J. Wheeler-Bennett, *Munich: prologue to tragedy*, London, 1948.

29 K. Middlemass, *The diplomacy of illusion: the British government and Germany, 1937–38*, London, 1971. Other critical accounts include L. W. Fuecher, *Neville Chamberlain and appeasement*, London, 1982; and W. Rock, *British appeasement in the 1930s*, London, 1977.

30 R. A. C. Parker, *Chamberlain and appeasement: British policy and the coming of the Second World War*, London, 1993.

31 Among the leading revisionists are Paul Kennedy and David Dilks. See P. Kennedy, 'Appeasement', in Martel (ed.), *Origins*; and D. Dilks, 'We must hope for the best and prepare for the worst: the prime minister, the cabinet and Hitler's Germany, 1937–39', *Proceedings of the British Academy* (1987). New thinking on appeasement is discussed extensively in W. J. Mommsen and L. Kettenacker (eds.), *The fascist challenge and the problem of appeasement*, London, 1983.

32 See J. Charmley, *Chamberlain, the lost peace*, London, 1989; and M. Cowling, *The impact of Hitler: British politics and British policy, 1933–39*, London, 1975.

33 See, for example, Taylor, *Origins*.

34 For a full discussion of research on French foreign policy during the inter-war period, see R. J. Young, *French foreign policy, 1918–45: a guide to research and research materials*, Wilmington, 1981; and R. J. Young, *France and the origins of the Second World War*, London, 1996.

35 A. Adamthwaite, *France and the coming of the Second World War*, London, 1977.

36 J-B. Duroselle, *La décadence, 1932–39: politique étrangère de la France*, Paris, 1979, pp. 10–30, 354–58.

37 R. Girault, 'The impact of the economic situation on the foreign policy of France, 1936–39', in Mommsen and Kettenacker (eds.), *The fascist challenge*.

38 See R. Frankenstein, 'The decline of France and French appeasement policies, 1936–39', in Mommsen and Kettenacker (eds.), *The fascist challenge*.

39 See, for example, R. Young, 'A. J. P. Taylor and the problem with France', in Martel (ed.), *Origins*.

40 *Ibid.*

41 R. Henig, *The origins of the Second World War*, London, p. 44.

42 R. J. Young, *In command of France: French foreign policy and military planning, 1933–40*, Cambridge, Mass. 1978.

43 For a detailed discussion of the historical debate on Mussolini's foreign policy, see S. Azzi, 'The historiography of fascist foreign policy', *Historical Journal*, vol. 36, no. 1 (1993).

44 G. Salvemeni, *Prelude to World War II*, London, 1953.

45 E. Wiskemann, *The Rome–Berlin Axis: a history of relations between Hitler and Mussolini*, London, 1949, p. 339.

46 D. Mack Smith, *Mussolini's Roman Empire*, London, 1976.

47 For a discussion of Taylor's view of Mussolini and its significance, see A. Cassels, 'Switching partners: Italy', in Martel (ed.), *Origins*. See also MacGregor Knox, 'The fascist regime and its wars: an anti-fascist orthodoxy', *Contemporary European History*, vol. 4, no. 3 (1995).

48 MacGregor Knox, *Mussolini unleashed, 1939–41: politics and strategy in fascist Italy's last war*, Cambridge, 1982.

49 G. Baer, *The coming of the Italian–Ethiopian War*, Cambridge, Mass. 1967.

50 For a discussion of De Felice's arguments, see MacGregor Knox, 'The fascist regime'.

51 A. Cassels, *Mussolini's early diplomacy*, Princeton, 1971.

52 D. C. Watt, 'The Rome–Berlin Axis, 1936–40: myth and reality', *The Review of Politics*, vol. 22 (1960).

53 P. Morgan, 'The Italian fascist new order in Europe', in M. L. Smith and P. M. R. Stirk (eds.), *The making of the new Europe? European unity and the Second World War*, London, 1990.

54 For a discussion of the current state of the historical debate on the Soviet Union and the origins of the Second World War, see G. Roberts, *The Soviet Union and the origins of the Second World War: Russo-German relations and the road to war, 1933–41*, London, 1995, pp. 1–8.

55 For a discussion of Taylor's view, see T. J. Uldricks, 'A. J. P. Taylor and the Russians', in Martel (ed.), *Origins*.

56 Two key supporters of the 'collective-security approach' are Roberts, *The Soviet Union*, and T. J. Uldricks, 'Soviet security policy in the 1930s', in G. Gorodetsky (ed.), *Soviet foreign policy, 1917–91*, London, 1991.

57 J. Haslam, *The Soviet Union and the struggle for collective security in Europe, 1933–39*, London, 1984.

58 *Ibid.*

59 W. Langer and S. Everett Gleason, 'Cold-War era revision: Stalin's "blank cheque" of 1939', in Snell (ed.), *Outbreak*.

60 See, for example, R. Tucker, 'The emergence of Stalin's foreign policy', *Slavic Review*, vol. 36 (1977).

61 The leading figures of the 'German school' are J. Hochmann, *The Soviet Union and the failure of collective security, 1934–38*, Ithaca, 1984; O. Pick 'Who pulled the trigger? Soviet historians and the origins of World War II', *Problems of Communism*, vol. 17 (1968); and G. Weinberg, *The foreign policy of Hitler's Germany*, 2 vols., Chicago, 1970, 1980.

62 E. Topitsch, *Stalin's war: a radical new theory on the origins of the Second World War*, London, 1987. See also N. Tolstoy, *Stalin's secret war*, London, 1981, for a similarly critical view of Stalin's foreign policy.

63 P. M. H. Bell, 'Fifty years on: some recent books on the coming of the Second World War in Europe', *Historical Journal*, vol. 32 (1989).

64 The leading supporter of the 'internal politics' approach is Haslam, *The Soviet Union*.

65 Hildebrand, *Foreign policy*.

66 J. Joll, *Europe since 1870*, London, 1973, p. 298.

67 Taylor, *Origins*, pp. 50, 336.

68 P. M. H. Bell, *The origins of the Second World War in Europe*, London, 1986, p. 29.

69 A. Lentin, *The Versailles Peace Conference: peacemaking with Germany*, London, 1991.

70 Historians who offer a sympathetic view of the 1919 peace settlement include A. Adamthwaite, *The lost peace: international relations, 1918–39*, London, 1980; R. Henig, *Versailles and after, 1919–33*, London, 1984; P. Kennedy, *The rise and fall of the great powers: economic change and military conflict*, London, 1988; G. Ross, *The great powers and the decline of the European states system, 1914–45*, London, 1983; and M. Trachtenberg, 'Versailles after sixty years', *Journal of Contemporary History*, vol. 16 (1982).

71 R. Overy, *The origins of the Second World War*, London, 1987, p. 27.

72 For a discussion of Marxist views, see Kershaw, *The Nazi dictatorship*.

73 See H. A. Turner, *German big business and the rise of Hitler*, Oxford, 1985.

74 T. Mason, 'The primacy of power-politics and economics in National Socialist Germany', in Henry A. Turner (ed.), *Nazism and the Third Reich*, New York, 1972.

75 Hildebrand, *Third Reich*.

76 W. Carr, *Arms, autarchy and aggression: a study of German foreign policy, 1933–39*, London, 1979.

77 See note 81.

78 See, for example, R. Overy, 'Germany, "domestic crisis", and the war in 1939', *Past and Present*, no. 116 (1987).

79 H. Arendt, *The origins of totalitarianism*, New York, 1951.

80 See, for example, R. Griffin, *The nature of fascism*, London, 1991; E. Weber, *Varieties of fascism*, New York, 1964; and S. Woolfe (ed.), *European fascism*, London, 1968.

81 G. Barrington Moore, *Social origins of dictatorship: lord and peasant in the making of the modern world*, London, 1966.

82 This sort of argument is advanced in H. Feis, *The road to Pearl Harbour*, Princeton, 1950.

83 For a discussion of recent trends within the historical debate, see N. J. Brailey, 'Southeast Asia and Japan's road to war', *Historical Journal*, vol. 30 (1987).

84 *The road to the Pacific war* originally appeared in Japan between 1962 and 1964. However, many of the documents in the study can be found in an English translation: see J. Morley (ed.), *Japan's road to the Pacific War*, 4 vols., New York, 1976–1984. For a detailed discussion of the Japanese documents, see A. Iriye, 'Japanese imperialism and aggression: reconsiderations II' and 'Japan's foreign policies between world wars: sources and interpretations', both in Robertson, (ed.), *Origins*.

85 A. Iriye, *The origins of the Second World War in Asia and the Pacific*, Harlow, 1987. See also A. Iriye, 'The Asian factor', in Martel (ed.), *Origins*.

86 Hosoya's view can be found in J. Morley (ed.), *Japan's road to war: the fateful choice*, vol. 4, New York, 1980.

87 See J. B. Crowley, *Japan's quest for autonomy: national security and foreign policy, 1930–38*, Princeton, 1966.

88 R. Devine, *The reluctant belligerent: American entry into World War II*, London, 1965, p. 158.

89 P. Schroeder, *The Axis alliance and Japanese–American relations*, Ithaca, New York, 1958. A series of critical views on Roosevelt's policy in the run-up to war have appeared regularly over the years. For a full discussion of the revisionist position, see R. Ferrell, 'Pearl Harbour and the revisionists' in Robertson (ed.), *Origins*. Those critics of Roosevelt include Charles A. Beard, Charles Tansill, William Chamberlain and Harry Elmer Barnes.

90 H. Elmer Barnes (ed.), *Perpetual war for perpetual peace*, Caldwell, 1953. This collection of essays is deeply critical of Roosevelt's actions in 1941.

91 Ferrell, 'Pearl Harbour', in Robertson (ed.), *Origins*.

Select bibliography

The available literature on the origins of the First and Second World Wars is enormous. Those studying the topic in greater depth are recommended to consult the very extensive and detailed sets of notes at the end of each chapter which give details of more specialised reading on the key issues and themes discussed in each chapter. The following list is confined to a selection of important books which offer a broad understanding of the subject.

The origins of the First World War

Introductory and general

There are a great many introductory texts. The most useful are R. Henig, *The origins of the First World War*, London, 1989; J. Joll, *The origins of the First World War*, London, 1984; H. W. Koch (ed.), *The origins of the First World War: great power rivalry and German war aims*, 2nd edn, London, 1984; and G. Martel, *The origins of the First World War*, 2nd edn, London, 1995. For a very detailed analysis of the historical debate, see J. Langdon, *July 1914: the long debate, 1918–90*, Oxford, 1991.

Individual countries

A great deal of attention has focused on the road to war in each of the major nations involved in the conflict. For the role of Germany, see V. R. Berghahn, *Germany and the approach of war in 1914*, London, 1973. For the role of Britain, look at Z. Steiner, *Britain and the origins of the First World War*, London, 1977. For France, see J. F. C. Kieger, *France and the origins of the First World War*, London, 1983. For Russia, consult D. C. B. Leiven, *Russia and the origins of the First World War*, London, 1983. For Austria-Hungary, see S. R. Williamson, *Austria-Hungary and the coming of the First World War*, London, 1990. For the Italian role, see R. J. B. Bosworth, *Italy and the approach of the First World War*, London, 1983.

Original documents

There are many detailed collections of original sources on the origins of the First World War. The standard collection remains I. Geiss (ed.), *July 1914: the outbreak of war: selected documents*, London, 1967.

The origins of the Second World War

Introductory and general

There are many useful introductory texts, but the following are strongly recommended: A. Adamthwaite, *The making of the Second World War*, London, 1977; P. M. H. Bell, *The origins of the Second World War*, London, 1986; R. Henig, *The origins of the Second World War*, London, 1985; A. Iriye, *The origins of the Second World War in the Asia-Pacific*, London, 1987; R. Overy, *The origins of the Second World War*, London, 1987; E. Robertson (ed.), *The origins of the Second World War*, London, 1971; A. J. P. Taylor, *The origins of the Second World War*, London, 1961; and D. C. Watt, *How war came*, London, 1989.

Individual countries

The following books deal with the road to war in each of the major nations involved in the conflict. For the role of Hitler and Nazi Germany, see I. Kershaw, *The Nazi dictatorship: problems and perspectives in interpretation*, 3rd edn, London, 1983; J. Hiden and J. Farquharson, *Explaining Hitler's Germany: historians and the Third Reich*, London, 1983; and K. Hildebrand, *The foreign policy of the Third Reich*, London, 1973. For the role of Chamberlain and British foreign policy, consult F. McDonough, *Neville Chamberlain, appeasement and the British path to war, 1918–39*, Manchester, 1997; R. A. C. Parker, *Chamberlain, appeasement and the coming of war*, London, 1993; and W. Rock, *British appeasement in the 1930s*, London, 1977. For the role of France, see A. Adamthwaite, *France and the coming of the Second World War*, London, 1977; and R. J. Young, *France and the origins of the Second World War*, London, 1996. For Mussolini and Italy, see B. M. Knox, *Mussolini unleashed, 1939–41: politics and strategy in Italy's last war*, Cambridge, 1982; and D. Mack Smith, *Mussolini*, London, 1981. For the role of the Soviet Union, see J. Haslam, *The Soviet Union and the struggle for collective security, 1933–39*, London, 1984; and G. Roberts, *The Soviet Union and the origins of the Second World War*, London, 1995. For the role of Japan, see I. Nish, *Japanese foreign policy, 1869–1942*, London, 1977. For the role of Roosevelt and the USA, consult R. A. Dallek, *Franklin D. Roosevelt and American foreign policy, 1932–45*, Oxford, 1979.

Original documents

There is a wide range of original document collections, but the following collections in English are worth consulting: N. H. Baynes (ed.), *The speeches of Adolf Hitler*, 2 vols., Oxford, 1942; C. Ciano, *Ciano's diary*, 2 vols., London, 1942, 1947; *Documents on British foreign policy*, 2nd series, vols. 1–19, 3rd series, vols. 1–9, London, 1946–82; *Documents on German foreign policy*, series C, vols. 1–6, series D, vols. 1–13, London, 1949–82; and J. Grenville (ed.), *The major international treaties, 1914–73*, London, 1974.

Chronology

1871   The German Empire is established. Wilhelm I of Prussia is proclaimed German emperor (Kaiser) and Otto von Bismarck chancellor.

1878   *13 July:* the Treaty of Berlin is signed.

1879   *7 October:* Austria-Hungary and Germany sign the Dual Alliance.

1882   *20 May:* the Triple Alliance of Germany, Austria-Hungary and Italy is formed.

1884   The Berlin West Africa Conference decides on a 'peaceful' partition of Africa.

1887   *18 June:* the secret Re-insurance Treaty between Germany and Russia is signed.

1888   Wilhelm I of Germany dies and is succeeded by Crown Prince Frederick. Frederick dies, and is succeeded by Crown Prince Wilhelm as German emperor (Wilhelm II).

1890   Otto von Bismarck is dismissed by Kaiser Wilhelm II, and is replaced by General Leo von Caprivi as German chancellor.
The Re-insurance Treaty between Germany and Russia is not renewed.

1894   *4 January:* the Franco-Russian Treaty is signed.
Von Caprivi resigns as German chancellor and is replaced by the relatively unknown Prince Hohenlohe-Schillingfurst.

1897   Count Bernhard von Bülow becomes German prime minister and in 1900 is appointed chancellor.
The Kaiser announces that Germany will follow a world policy (*Weltpolitik*) designed to make the new empire a major international power.
Admiral von Tirpitz is appointed German secretary of state for the navy, with the aim of building a 'world-class navy'.

1898   *28 March:* the German Reichstag approves the first Navy Law.
16 July: the Fashoda Crisis between Britain and France ends in a French climbdown.

1899   *11 October:* the Boer War begins (and ends in a British victory in 1902).

1900   *12 June:* the German Reichstag approves the second Navy Law.

1902   *30 January:* the Anglo-Japanese Treaty is signed.

1904   *8 February:* the outbreak of the Russo-Japanese War (ends in a surprise Japanese victory in 1905).
8 April: the Anglo-French Entente is signed.

1905   *31 March:* German navy sails into Tangier and sparks the first Moroccan Crisis between Germany and France.
October: HMS *Dreadnought*, a new, British state-of-the-art battleship is launched.

1906   *January–April:* the Algeciras Conference opens. France, with the support of Britain and Russia, gains major economic concessions in Morocco.

The German Reichstag approves the third Navy Law. Germany decides to produce its own dreadnought-style battleship. The Anglo-German naval race begins.

1907 *31 August:* the Anglo-Russian Convention is signed.

1908 *6 October:* Austria-Hungary annexes Bosnia-Herzegovina. Kaiser Wilhelm II supports Austria-Hungary in 'shining armour'. Russian and Serbian nationalists are outraged.

1909 Theobald von Bethmann Hollweg is appointed German chancellor.

1911 French troops occupy Fez, and are warned by Germany that they are infringing the Algeciras agreement.

1 July: The German gunboat *Panther* steams into Agadir to spark the second Moroccan Crisis.

21 July: Lloyd George, British chancellor of the exchequer, warns Germany in his famous Mansion House speech that Britain will stand by France in the Agadir Crisis.

4 November: an agreement on Morocco is signed. Germany agrees to France gaining a 'free hand' in Morocco in return for part of French Congo.

1912 Kaiser Wilhelm II announces major spending increases in the German army and navy. The Balkan League is formed.

8 October: the First Balkan War begins between Turkey and Bulgaria, Serbia and Greece (and ends in a Turkish defeat).

1913 *29 June:* the Second Balkan War begins. Bulgaria attacks Serbia and Greece, but a coalition consisting of Serbia, Greece, Turkey and Romania easily defeat Bulgaria.

1914 *28 June:* the assassination of Archduke Franz Ferdinand in Sarajevo sparks the 'July Crisis'.

5 July: Kaiser Wilhelm II gives Austria-Hungary a 'blank cheque' to deal with Serbia.

23 July: Austria-Hungary sends an ultimatum to Serbia.

28 July: Austria-Hungary declares war on Serbia.

31 July: Russia orders a general mobilisation of its army.

1 August: Germany declares war on Russia and France, and sends an ultimatum to Belgium, which is rejected.

3 August: Germany declares war on France, and France declares war on Germany.

Italy decides to remain neutral.

German troops invade Belgium.

4 August: Britain declares war on Germany.

1917 *October:* the Russian Revolution establishes the first 'Workers' state' led by V. I. Lenin, leader of the Marxist-inspired Bolshevik Party.

1918 *March:* Germany and Russia sign the Treaty of Brest-Litovsk

11 November: Germany signs an armistice to end the 'Great War'.

1919 *19 January:* the Paris Peace Conference decides how Germany and its allies are to be treated, and how a second world war can be prevented.

February: the League of Nations is set up by the peacemakers to preserve peace and to prevent future wars by negotiation.

26 June: the Treaty of Versailles is signed by Germany under protest. Germany must pay £6,600 million in war costs and accept guilt for starting the First World War.

1923 The 'great inflation' in Germany sparks a currency crisis.

French troops occupy Belgium and the Ruhr to enforce the payment of reparations by Germany.

1924 *April:* the Dawes Plan is introduced. This is an American economic aid package, including a loan of 800 million gold marks, and is designed to ease the pressure on the German economy and to help in the payment of reparations. The German economy recovers, reparations are paid, and France agrees to withdraw troops from the Ruhr.

1925 *October:* the Locarno Treaty is signed. Germany agrees to the western frontiers decided at Versailles, but not its eastern frontiers. The treaty is regarded as a major reconciliation between Germany and France.

1926 *September:* Germany joins the League of Nations.

1928 *August:* the Kellogg–Briand Pact, under which 56 nations, including Germany, Italy, Britain, Soviet Union, France, Italy and Japan, agree to 'renounce war as a legitimate policy', is signed.

1929 *October:* the Young Plan is introduced, a second American economic aid plan aimed at Germany. It is virtually an admission by Britain and France that reparations have failed. The total reparations bill is reduced from £6,600 to £2,000 million.

The Wall Street stock-market crash in the USA sparks off the worst economic depression of the twentieth century.

1931 *September:* Japan occupies Manchuria. The League of Nations decides not to invoke either economic or military sanctions.

1932 The World Disarmament Conference opens (and ends in failure).

November: F. D. Roosevelt is elected US president.

1933 *30 January:* Hitler, leader of the ultra-nationalistic National Socialist Party (NSDAP), is appointed German chancellor.

February: Japan leaves the League of Nations following a request to remove its troops from Manchuria.

October: Germany leaves the League of Nations and walks out of the World Disarmament Conference.

1934 *September:* the Soviet Union joins the League of Nations.

1935 *16 March:* Hitler announces German repudiation of the arms-limitation clauses of the Treaty of Versailles. Conscription is introduced and naval and air programmes are announced.

April: the Stresa Front; Britain, France and Italy meet at Stresa in a move designed to halt further German rearmament.

21 June: the Anglo-German Naval Agreement allows Germany to build a navy 33 per cent of the strength of the British navy. France and Italy are outraged.

October: Italy invades Abyssinia. The League of Nations imposes economic sanctions (which are not successful).

December: the Hoare–Laval Pact. Britain and France secretly agree to accept the Italian invasion of Abyssinia. News of the agreement leaks to the press. Samuel Hoare, the British foreign secretary, is forced to resign, and is replaced by Anthony Eden, a firm supporter of the League of Nations.

1936 *7 March:* German troops reoccupy the Rhineland. The League of Nations takes no action. The Locarno Treaty is destroyed.

17 July: the Spanish Civil War begins. Italy and Germany offer military support to General Franco, the fascist leader, and the Soviet Union offers aid to the Popular Front. Britain and France adopt a policy of non-intervention. The civil war ends in victory for Franco on 1 April 1939.

October: the Rome–Berlin Axis is signed. Italy is now an ally of Hitler.

November: Germany signs the Anti-Comintern Pact with Japan (which is later signed by Italy), which pledges to fight 'the world-wide communist conspiracy'.

1937 *28 May:* Chamberlain becomes British prime minister and pledges to support a 'policy of appeasement' towards Nazi Germany and Italy.

July: war breaks out between Japan and China.

1938 *20 February:* Eden resigns as British foreign secretary, claiming 'fundamental differences' with Chamberlain over the likely success of appeasement.

12 March: Germany moves into Austria in the *Anschluss.*

August: Chamberlain sends Lord Runciman to Czechoslovakia to discuss the grievances of its Germany minority in the Sudetenland.

15 September: Chamberlain visits Hitler in Germany to try to find a peaceful solution to the Czech crisis.

30 September: the Munich Agreement; Britain, Germany, France and Italy agree to transfer the Sudetenland to Germany. Czechoslovakia and the Soviet Union are not invited to participate in the talks.

1 October: Chamberlain proclaims that the Munich Agreement has brought 'peace in our time'.

1939 *15 March:* Germany invades Czechoslovakia. Hitler claims that German troops were invited to 'keep order'.

31 March: Britain and France offer a guarantee to defend Poland from a German attack. Similar assurances are given to Greece, Romania and Turkey.

May–August: Britain attempts to gain an Anglo-Soviet agreement.

22 May: Hitler and Mussolini sign the 'Pact of Steel' – a military alliance.

23 August: Hitler and Stalin sign the Nazi–Soviet Pact offering mutual assurances of non-aggression.

1 September: Germany invades Poland.

3 September: Britain and France declare war on Germany. Italy remains neutral.

1940 *10 May:* Chamberlain is replaced by Churchill as British prime minister.

June: France is defeated in less than five weeks by Germany.

August–September: Britain repels a German air assault in the Battle of Britain and stands alone, for nearly a year, against Germany.

1941 *22 June:* Germany invades the Soviet Union.

7 December: Japan launches a surprise attack on the US fleet at Pearl Harbour. The USA enters the war.

Index